New Education Policy 2020: Paradigm Shift in Higher Education

New Education Policy 2020: Paradigm Shift in Higher Education

Editors

Dr. Apilang Apum

&

Dr. Sony Dupak

KALPAZ

Published by

KALPAZ

Kalpaz Publications
C-30, Satyawati Nagar,
Delhi – 110052
Ph.: 011-47034999, 9811692060
www.kalpazpublications.com
E-mail: kalpaz@hotmail.com

Distribution Network

gyanbooks.com

India, USA, Canada, UK, Australia, France

ISBN: 978-93-5722-519-9 (HB)
First Published, 2025

Printed at: Gyan Press, Delhi.

New Education Policy 2020: Paradigm Shift in Higher Education
Editors: DR. APILANG APUM & DR. SONY DUPAK

Contents

Foreword

The transformation of education is a continuous process that acclimates to the changing needs of society, technology, and the economy. The National Education Policy (NEP) 2020, with its comprehensive and ingenious approach, marks an indispensable moment of India's educational landscape.

The thirteen articles in this volume are a collection of papers delivered during a national seminar on "National Education Policy 2020: Paradigm Shift in Higher Education," jointly organised by the Department of Education and the Department of Economics, Jawaharlal Nehru College, Pasighat, on March 12, 2024. Through the lens of NEP 2020, the papers focus on the implications, challenges, and opportunities that exist in various facets of education. The collection explores a wide range of aspects of the policy, including its impact on higher education, teacher training, and employability, its role in the promotion of vocational education, ICT integration, and the preservation and cultural heritage through folktales.

The present collection, through a detailed analysis of the policy's shift from the National Policy on Education 1986, further provides insights into the fundamental changes that are shaping India's education system in the 21st century. Special attention is also given to the unique challenges faced by regions like Arunachal Pradesh, where the implementation of NEP 2020 can bring about remarkable socio-economic and educational progress.

As we stand on the threshold of a new era in education, this book seeks to serve as a worthy resource for educators, policymakers, students, and researchers. The insights shared in the book furnish a nuanced understanding of the NEP 2020, thereby contribute to the ongoing discourse on education reforms and the collaborative effort to overcome obstacles and fully realise the vision of a more inclusive, equitable, and progressive education system in India.

Prof. Anga Padu

Dept. of Education
Rajiv Gandhi University

Acknowledgments

This book is based on the papers presented in the National Seminar on 'New Education Policy 2020: Paradigm Shift in Higher Education' organised by the Department of Education and Economics, Jawaharlal Nehru College, Pasighat in collaboration with Doying Gumin Government College Pasighat on 12th March 2024. We are thankful to the Director of Higher & Technical Education, Government of Arunachal Pradesh, Doying Gumin College Pasighat and Jawaharlal Nehru College Pasighat for providing the financial support in organising the National Seminar. Our heartful thanks also goes to all the faculty members of the Department of Education and Economics, Jawaharlal Nehru College Pasighat for their cooperation and assistance during the seminar. We are also thankful to the under graduate students of the Department of Education and Economics, Jawaharlal Nehru College for extending help in various capacities during the seminar. Last but not the least, we are grateful to all the paper contributors without whom this edited volume would never have been published.

Editorial Board

List of Contributors

Bijaya Das, Research Scholar, Apex Professional University, Pasighat, Arunachal Pradesh

Duyir Poyom, Guest Assistant Professor, Dept. of Education, Donyi Polo Govt. College, Kamki

Elina Mossang, Research Scholar, Department of Education, Rajiv Gandhi University, Rono Hills, Doimukh, Arunachal Pradesh

Gamter Ori, Assistant Professor, Dept. of English, Donyi Polo Government College, Kamki

Geyin Miyu, Ma Iv Semester, Department of Education, Rajiv Gandhi University, Itanagar

Haj Morney, Guest Assistant Professor, Dept. of Hindi, Donyi Polo Govt. College

Kangkana Barman, Lecturer, Faculty of Law & Forensic Sciences, Apex Professional University, Pasighat, Arunachal Pradesh

Kigo Riksap, Ma Iv Semester, Department of Education, Rajiv Gandhi University, Itanagar

Ligang Suniya, Assistant Professor, Dept of Education, Donyi Polo Government College, Kamki

Luina Boruah, Ma Iv Semester, Department of Education, Rajiv Gandhi University, Itanagar

Mumni Tayeng, Research Scholar, Department of Education, Rajiv Gandhi University, Itanagar

Neena Hamid, Senior Assistant, Acharya Faculty of Law & Forensic Sciences, Apex Professional University, Pasighat, Arunachal Pradesh

Oman Taloh, Asst Prof., Dept. of Economics, J.N. College, Pasighat

Poonam Subedi, Research Scholar, Department of Education, Rajiv Gandhi University, Itanagar

Ruma Nalo, Ma Iv Semester, Department of Education, Rajiv Gandhi University, Itanagar

Sushant Kumar Nayak, Assistant Professor, Department of Education Rajiv Gandhi University, Rono Hills, Doimukh, Arunachal Pradesh

Tony Jamoh, Assistant Professor, Department of Education, J.N. College, Pasighat, Arunachal Pradesh

Yab Anu Comdir, Ma Iv Semester, Department of Education, Rajiv Gandhi University, Itanagar

Yuton Lhamu, Assistant Professor, Department of Education, Binni Yanga Government Women's College, Lekhi, Naharlagun.

Introduction

The NEP 2020 outlines a variety of reforms and initiatives to cultivate a more inclusive and flexible education system. The policy foresees a transition to a multi-disciplinary learning approach, giving prominence to skill development, critical thinking, creativity, and the seamless integration of technology. It promotes an atmosphere conducive to innovation and research within higher education, which plays a pivotal role in shaping India as a democratic, just, socially conscious, cultured, and compassionate society by the vision outlined in its Constitution. Acknowledging the knowledge economy of the 21st century and the increasing aspiration for higher education, the NEP 2020 envisions positioning India as a global educational leader. It provides an opportunity for Higher Educational Institutions (HEIs), especially those in technical education, to contribute directly to transforming the country into a global knowledge superpower. The policy aspires to create an inclusive and equitable education system, introducing broad based, multi-disciplinary, and flexible education at the higher education level. The present edited volume seeks to highlight key issues related to NEP 2020 by encouraging scholarly discourse to promote its objectives and share innovative ideas within the academic community.

A total of thirteen research papers added a valuable insight into various aspects and challenges of National Education Policy (NEP) 2020 in India and Arunachal Pradesh. In Chapter I, **Barman** provides an analytical study on the impact of the National Education Policy (NEP) 2020 on transforming the higher education system in India to a holistic and multidisciplinary approach, with the goal of establishing

India as a global knowledge superpower. **Naren and Luina** in Chapter II highlights the fact that the National Education Policy (NEP) 2020 represents a significant paradigm shift in higher education in India, particularly with regard to the integration of information and communication technology (ICT) to enhance accessibility, quality, and inclusivity in education. In Chapter III, **Poonam and Sushant** provides a comparative analysis of the national education policy (nep) 2020 and the previous National Policy on Education (NPE) 1986, highlighting the key similarities and differences between the two policies. In Chapter IV, **Neena** discusses the National Education Policy 2020 (NEP 2020) and its vision to transform the Indian education system to meet the needs of 21st century India, with a focus on flexibility, interdisciplinary learning, and holistic development of students. In Chapter V, **Oman** discusses the trends in budgetary allocation and expenditure in the higher education sector in India, as well as the key highlights of the National Education Policy (NEP) 2020 and its impact on higher education.

In Chapter VI, **Ligang, Haj and Duyir** discusses the need for a holistic and multidisciplinary education in Higher Education Institutions in Arunachal Pradesh, India as envisioned by the National Education Policy(NEP) 2020, and the challenges in implementing this approach.

In Chapter VII, **Geyin** reflects the issues and challenges of teacher's education in India, particularly in the light of the National Education Policy (NEP) 2020, which aims to transform the education system, including higher education, by focusing on multidisciplinary education, flexibility in curriculum, and promoting research. In **Chapter VIII, Yuton** discusses the challenges of teacher education in the context of the New Education Policy (NEP) 2020 in India, highlighting the need for reforms in the teacher education system to meet the changing demands of the education system. In Chapter IX, **Yab and Ruma** summarises the efforts made by the New Education Policy (NEP) 2020 to improve employability through higher education in India including the integration of vocational education into mainstream education, the development of skill-based programmes, and the collaboration between higher education institutions and industries. This paper highlights that NEP 2020 aims to integrate vocational education into mainstream education across all educational institutions in a phased manner and focuses on removing the social stigma associated with vocational education and integrating it into mainstream education system. In Chapter X, **Elina and Sushanta** explores the prospects and challenges of vocational education in Arunachal Pradesh within the context of the National Education Policy (NEP) 2020. Amidst rising youth unemployment, vocational education emerges as a crucial tool for addressing the state's economic challenges. The NEP 2020 underscores the importance of integrating vocational education into mainstream schooling, aiming to bridge the gap between academic knowledge and practical skills. The research analyses the impact of NEP 2020 on vocational education in Arunachal Pradesh, highlighting significant growth in enrollment rates and the implementation of skill development initiatives. Despite progress, challenges such as resource constraint and lack of awareness persist. The paper concludes that vocational education holds immense potential in empowering youth and fostering socio-economic development but emphasises the need for concerted efforts to overcome existing challenges and fully realise its benefits. In Chapter XI, **Tony** summarises the challenges in implementing the Common University Entrance Test (CUET) in Arunachal Pradesh under the National Education Policy (NEP) 2020, focusing on issues related to infrastructure, equity and accessibility. These challenges create barriers for students in remote areas, particularly affecting economically disadvantaged students who face additional costs for travel and accommodation. In Chapter XII, **Ligang and Gamter** examines the role of folktales in preserving cultural identity, transmitting moral values, and fostering a sense of community and environmental care, as well as their educational value in promoting critical thinking, creativity, and social-emotional learning. The study found that Folktales serve as a means to transmit cultural values and preserve cultural identity, language, and traditional knowledge. Folktales have positive benefits on children's socio-emotional development, language acquisition, and moral education.

There is a need to protect and document folktales to ensure their transmission to future generations, with parents and teachers playing a critical role in this process. In Chapter XIII, **Mumni and Nayak** provides an overview of the status of implementation of the National Education Policy (NEP) 2020 in Arunachal Pradesh, with a focus on school education, particularly Early Childhood Care and Education (ECCE) and Foundation Literacy and Numeracy (FLN)

Chapter - 1

An analytical study on impact of NEP 2020 on Higher Education in driving holistic education growth landscape in India

– *Kangkana Barman*

Abstract

Education is a vibrant driving force through which human beings are capable of developing their rational thought, talents and resources. The NEP 2020 is that policy which has been initiated to transform the Indian education system to a global context by adopting the Goal 4 (SDG4) of the 2030 Agenda for Sustainable Development in 2015. This research paper focuses on analytical investigation on the objectives of NEP 2020 in transforming Higher Education as one of its visions to a holistic and multidisciplinary institution. NEP 2020 emphasized on various key principles required for ensuring quality education to all and to establish a society with vibrant knowledge. Higher education institutions contribute to substantial development and promote lifelong learning to individuals, so the NEP 2020 ensures a significant and different role to Higher Education Institutions of India to create a global knowledge superpower.

This research paper will shed light on the challenges of Higher Education Institutions in robust implementation of NEP 2020 with a comparison to some of the education policies in the global environment for the purpose of developing India into a growing national economy. Through this study, the role of regulatory bodies to assure a check and balance into the powers and functions of Higher Education Institutions will also lead to institutional and academic upliftment of the education system will also be emphasized. Therefore, NEP 2020 envisions a true spirit not only in driving into a holistic development of Higher Education Institutions but overall development of youth of India to reach their desired goals. This policy will revamp the higher education structure into knowledge hubs through high quality teaching, research, skill and value based curriculum, community participation and this will overhaul the HEIs to overcome all the challenges of contemporary society and provide an inclusive education and greater opportunities of employability.

Keywords: NEP 2020, Sustainable Development, Higher Education Institutions (HEIs), Holistic and Multidisciplinary.

Introduction

Education is a process of life that every individual should accomplish to establish themselves firmly in the civilised society. Education deeply shows the path of knowledge and light for upbringing of human beings to burgeon as responsible citizens of the society. Knowledge is never ending and without knowledge or quality education an individual cannot prosper in life. India has always driven forward to universal access to quality education for rooting out rich talents and resources of the nation. Many national leaders and renowned thinkers have been positive since India got independence and a Supreme Constitution of the land, trying to focus and strengthen the education system of India. The National Education Policy (NEP) 2020 is a comprehensive and guiding light of eternal Indian Knowledge.

The first National Policy on Education, 1968 recommended 'radical reconstruction of education' for the socio-cultural and economic development of the country. The Sixth Five Year Plan (1980-1985) emphasized on universal primary education, illiteracy, and introduction of job prospects in the education system. The National Policy on Education 1986 marked the changes with the introduction of information technology and to provide education to all sections of the people. Further, the National Policy on Education (1992) also known as National Programme of Action 1992, emphasized the need for greater transformation of the Indian educational system, with a focus on quality enhancement of all learners in the country. It is a modified version of the policy of 1986 that highlighted quality education and accessibility to all along with providing the Constitutional right to free and compulsory education. The NEP 2020 was introduced after that which created a historical achievement by the Government of India in the education sector keeping in view the Sustainable Development Goal 4 of the 2030 Agenda for Sustainable Development, which seeks to "ensure inclusive and equitable quality education and promote lifelong learning opportunities for all" by 2030.

The NEP 2020 sets a vision based on Indian ethos and thoughts which will transfer all the learners into skilled, responsible and truly global citizens. It has laid down a sustainable education environment by emphasizing on the Indian knowledge system, value education, holistic development and inclusive quality education.

Transforming Higher Education into a holistic institution

A holistic approach of education is very much essential to transform the Higher Education system. Holistic approach means physical, social, moral, aesthetic and creative development. The term 'Holistic' originated from the Greek word 'Holism'. The concept of Holistic Education came into existence in the mid 1980s in North America with the growth of the Holistic Education Movement. The NEP 2020 envisages that holistic approach can be achieved only by converting the higher education institutions into holistic multidisciplinary education institutions with multiple entry/exit options creating flexibility and new possibilities for life-long learning. This will also lead to inclusiveness in higher education. Holistic approach will help in transforming the curriculum into an innovative and research oriented for the learners. Educational institutions are the 'wisdom of the crowds' where everyone has the potential to be an expert to access and use knowledge exclusively. Thus, a holistic approach will include in promoting life skills, community participation and research oriented structure of education.

The way forward for holistic development includes-

I. Introduction of Credit-based courses and projects in the areas of community engagement and service, environmental education, and value-based education.

II. Opportunities for internships with local industry, businesses, artists, crafts persons, and research internships for the students which will actively improve their employability.

III. Introduction of life skills like cooperation, teamwork, empathy, resilience in the curricula will help in overall development and progress of the learners.

IV. Guidelines for Multiple Entry and Exit in Academic Programmes offered in the HEIs have been issued on 29.07.2021 to pave the way for seamless student mobility, This initiative is taken to stem the dropout rate, improve GER by offering flexibility in curricula and novel course options to students in addition to discipline-specific specialisations, by facilitating the encashment of credits earned when the learner resumes his/her programmes of study. For this, the example of Academic Bank of Credit which should be established by HEIs to keep the degree and award records of the students digitally.

V. Curriculum and Credit Framework for Undergraduate Programmes has been issued on 12.12.2022 to set up a flexible choice-based credit system with a multidisciplinary approach. This will facilitate flexibility to move from one discipline of study to another, one institution to another, switch to alternative modes of learning (offline, ODL, & Online learning, and hybrid modes of learning), multiple entry and exit options with UG (certificate/diploma/degree) and to choose the courses of their interest in all disciplines. At present, 105 Universities have adopted it as per the data reported to UGC.

VI. The higher education system is characterised by quality of education, internalisation and institutional restructuring to build vibrant communities of learners.

VII. NEP 2020 has set a target to increase the current Gross Enrollment Ratio (GER) to 50% by 2035 and to achieve this there should be a rise in virtual learning and increased role of technology in higher education. Open Distance Learning and online programmes like MOOC and Swayam should be ensured with motivated faculty to enhance the enrollment ratio in the higher education institutions.

VIII. Guidelines for the establishment of Research and Development Cell (RDC) in universities and colleges have been issued on 04.03.2022. This cell in HEIs will enable attainment of targets of "Atma-Nirbhar Bharat" and is expected to play a pivotal role in catalyzing multidisciplinary/ trans-disciplinary and translational research culture. Around 2500 HEIs and 300 Universities have established R&D Cells at their campuses as per the current records.

Challenges of Higher Education Institutions in robust implementation of NEP 2020:

The NEP 2020 was enacted with the vision to re-energise the higher education system to overcome the challenges and ensure access, equity and inclusion in quality education to all without any disparity. However, the challenges that laminated in the higher education system are the following:

(a) The higher education institutions have to be transformed into vibrant multidisciplinary environments fostering local languages in every district. A university or college will be multidisciplinary when it will offer quality teaching, research innovation and community engagement in graduation courses to the learners. This will help in reducing language and cultural barriers.

(b) Promoting or uplifting faculty and institutional autonomy. The University Grants Commission (UGC) is entrusted with the power of giving greater flexibility towards academic development with regards to improvement of academic standards and excellence.

(c) "Light but tight" regulatory system under a single regulatory body for the control and assurance of transparency in distinct functions of higher education institutions.

As per All India Survey on Higher Education (AISHE) 2020-2021, the following achievements are made out in robust implementation of NEP 2020.

- Increase of 29% in Student Enrolment and 34% in Female Student Enrollment in the North-Eastern Region in 2020-2021 since 2014-2015.
- The Gross Enrollment in Distance Education has increased by 7% in 2020-2021 from the year 2019-20.
- The number of universities has increased by 70 and the number of colleges has increased by 1435 in 2020-21 as compared to 2019-20.
- The Gender Parity Index (GPI) has increased from 1 in 2017-2018 to 1.05 in 2020-2021.

If India has to establish a global knowledge hub, the NEP should focus attention on utilisation of novel technologies for education. It has been observed that modern technology has redefined the entire teaching and learning process in the higher education system. The American institutions use the latest technologies such as AI, IoT, Gaming, Virtual Reality, SLEs, etc. The NEP has envisaged use of modern technologies in education to the extent possible by the Digital India Campaign led by the Government of India. The NEP has further proposed that good American and European Universities can establish their Campuses in India so that Indians receive high quality education and research facilities at less cost, compared to full-time higher education abroad. This will ensure global quality standards and enrollment of a greater number of international students pursuing higher education.

The educational policy of China is innovation driven and whereas NEP 2020 aims at holistic development keeping its rootedness in Indian literature and culture.

Germany's higher education policy assures quality of research and teaching as the central task and emphasizes on the need to maintain the student-teacher ratio by proper accreditation study programmes. NEP 2020 created a single regulatory body for unification for academic accreditation and other relevant purposes.

The role of regulatory bodies to assure a check and balance into the powers and functions of Higher Education Institutions

A proper mechanism is the need of the educational institutions to re-energize the higher education sector and to check and balance powers and functions without any conflicts of interest. Inspite of various regulatory bodies, NEP 2020 has made the Higher Education Council (HECI) as the autonomous umbrella body to regulate the HEIs and to ensure transparency and efficiency constituted of eminent public-spirited experts in Higher Education. This regulatory regime is an initiative by the Government through the policy of 2020 assures the planned development process of higher education. The underlying principle behind a regulatory regime will be that of a faceless and transparent regulatory intervention using technology and without human intervention.

1. The HECI will have four distinct verticals under it for smooth regulation and to eradicate any kinds of flaws in the system.
2. National Higher Education Regulatory Council (NHERC) is the first body that will function as the single point regulator for investigating teacher education, excluding medical and legal education to eliminate the duplication and disjunction of regulatory efforts by the multiple regulatory agencies that exist at the present time.
3. National Accreditation Council (NAC), the second vertical will look into the Accreditation of institutions to set up a robust system of graded accreditation. All HEIs will aim, through their Institutional Development Plans (IDPs), to attain the highest level of accreditation over the next 15 years.

4. The third vertical of HECI will be the Higher Education Grants Council (HEGC), with the objective to carry out funding and financing of higher education. HEGC will have the power to disburse scholarships and developmental funds for launching new focus areas and expanding quality programme offerings at HEIs.
5. The fourth vertical of HECI will be the General Education Council (GEC), which will formulate a National Higher Education Qualification Framework (NHEQF) in connection with the National Skills Qualifications Framework (NSQF) to ease the integration of vocational education into higher education. It will identify specific skills that students must acquire during their academic programmes to prepare themselves as well-rounded learners with 21st century skills and potentialities.

Therefore, this regulatory framework will assure the true spirit of autonomy, good governance and sequential criteria for composed functioning of the HEIs.

Conclusions and Suggestions

Conclusions

The NEP 2020 is an enhanced landmark document designed by the Government of India to make huge reform and revamp India i.e. Bharat into a global superpower knowledge hub. This initiative of the government is truly remarkable in the history of India because it has opened many paths to achieve all the challenges of education by the learners of our society. It has observed that India being an old civilisation hosted by renowned scholars contributed towards the culture and philosophy of India.

This policy is implemented with the objective to open up a new world to the learners by enabling them life-long learning opportunities through holistic structure of education. The NEP 2020 has been set up to upgrade the curriculum pedagogy by introducing vocational courses, multidisciplinary institutions, graded autonomy, quality education by motivated faculty, enhanced infrastructure and extensive use of technological methods in the pursuit of higher education.

Higher education is a significant part of the education system as it leads to overall development and progress of an individual. It lays the foundation of a social and dignified life. So, it is a matter of high concern that through this policy initiatives are taken for the proper and full-fledged implementation of it so that society can be benefited and stimulate appropriate opportunities for its progress and livelihood.

Therefore, it may be concluded that the NEP 2020 recognizes the capabilities and creativeness of individual learners through higher education. It establishes the root of the higher education system by giving importance to the ethical and constitutional principles and values for the inclusive development of the present and future generation.

Suggestions

- A proper implementation of NEP 2020 is required to achieve the objectives of this policy for the socio-economic benefits.
- The higher education sector should significantly ensure a holistic approach for flexibility of the learners and increase the enrollment rate.
- Multidisciplinary institutions should be established for quality education and to maintain unity and integrity of all knowledge that our country is devoid of.
- Research innovative techniques and courses should be full-fledgedly introduced in the universities for upgrading and outstanding enrichment of knowledge.
- Provision of autonomous regulatory regime in higher education institutions will foster transparency, accountability and integrity.
- Every HEIs must be concerned about the interests and career prospects of the students to ensure a holistic environment.

As this will not only increase the enrollment rate but also the employability potentiality of the youth in our societies.

References

Bania, Shisira, East African Scholars Journal of Education, Humanities and Literature, "*National Education Policy-2020 & Institutional Autonomy in Indian Higher Education System: Issues and Challenges in Implementation*," Volume-4, Issue-6, June- 2021.

https://www.education.gov.in/sites/upload_files/mhrd/files/document-reports/NPE-1968.pdf. Accessed 3 March 2024

https://www.egyankosh.ac.in/bitstream/123456789/71552/1/Unit-3.pdf Accessed 3 March 2024

https://www.education.gov.in/nep/multidisciplinary-holistic-education Accessed 7 March 2024

https://iucee.org/wp-content/uploads/2021/05/NEP-HE-Guidelines.pdf Assessed 7 March 2024

https://static.pib.gov.in/WriteReadData/specificdocs/documents/2023/jul/doc2023726228501.pdf Assessed 8 March 2024

https://static.pib.gov.in/WriteReadData/specificdocs/documents/2023/jul/doc2023726228501.pdf Assessed 8 March 2024

https://static.pib.gov.in/WriteReadData/specificdocs/documents/2023/jul/doc2023726228501.pdf Assessed 8 March 2024

https://pib.gov.in/PressReleseDetailm.aspx?PRID=1894517 Assessed 8 March 2024.

Singh, Pratima, Developing a Teacher Training Model Based on Holistic Approach for Teaching English, 2019

Ramesh, Ms. Sujatha and Natarajan, Dr. K., International Journal of Humanities and Social Science Invention (IJHSSI), New Education Policy of India: A Comparative Study with the Education System of USA, |Volume 8 Issue 06 Ser. III, 2019)

Chapter - 2

National Education Policy, 2020: Paradigm Shift in Higher Education with reference to Information and Communication Technology (ICT)

– Mr. Naren Borah, Ms. Luina Boruah

Abstract

The National Education Policy (NEP) 2020 heralds a transformative shift in higher education, particularly in its approach to integrating Information and Communication Technology (ICT). The NEP 2020 encapsulates a vision of holistic and flexible learning, underpinned by digital innovation. It emphasizes leveraging ICT to foster personalised and adaptive learning experiences, transcending geographical barriers and catering to diverse learner needs. NEP 2020 advocates for the development of digital infrastructure and resources to democratize access to quality education, empowering learners of all backgrounds. Moreover, it underscores the importance of digital literacy, equipping students with essential skills for the 21st century workforce. The policy envisions a dynamic ecosystem where technology enhances pedagogy, assessment, and administrative processes, driving continuous improvement in higher education institutions. Embracing a learner-centric approach, NEP 2020 encourages the creation of digital content and platforms that promote self-directed learning and lifelong education. By embracing ICT as a catalyst for innovation and inclusivity, NEP 2020 lays the foundation for a vibrant higher education landscape that is responsive to the evolving needs of society and the economy. Therefore, this paper aim to discuss paradigm shift in higher education with reference to ICT based on the secondary sources of information.

Key words: National Education Policy, 2020, Paradigm Shift, Higher Education, Information and Communication Technology.

Introduction

The National Education Policy (NEP) 2020 represents a significant paradigm shift in higher education, particularly regarding Information and Communication Technology (ICT). Introduced as a comprehensive framework by the Government of India, NEP 2020 aims to revolutionize the education landscape by integrating ICT across all levels of learning. This policy emphasizes leveraging digital tools and platforms to enhance accessibility, quality, and inclusivity in education. NEP 2020 acknowledges ICT as a cornerstone in fostering innovation, collaboration, and personalised learning experiences. It advocates for the integration of ICT tools such as online learning platforms, virtual classrooms, and educational apps to supplement traditional teaching methods. Moreover, the policy underscores the importance of ICT infrastructure development, digital literacy, and teacher training programmes to effectively harness the potential of technology in education. By promoting the widespread adoption of ICT, NEP 2020 seeks to address various challenges in higher education, including geographical barriers, resource constraints, and outdated pedagogical practices. It envisions a dynamic learning ecosystem where students can access high-quality educational resources anytime, anywhere, thereby democratizing education and empowering learners to thrive in the digital age.

NEP 2020 also emphasizes the integration of emerging technologies such as artificial intelligence, machine learning, and data analytics into higher education curricula. By incorporating these cutting-edge technologies, the policy aims to equip students with the necessary skills to navigate and succeed in a rapidly evolving digital economy. Furthermore, NEP 2020 encourages the establishment of interdisciplinary research centers and collaborations with industry partners to foster innovation and entrepreneurship in ICT-related fields. This approach not only enriches academic learning but also promotes the development of practical solutions to real-world problems, driving economic growth and societal progress. The objectives of this paper are to discuss paradigm shift in higher education with reference to ICT based on the secondary sources of information. For construction of this paper we used descriptive method. Overall, the introduction of NEP 2020 heralds a new era of transformation in higher education, where ICT plays a central role in driving excellence, equity, and relevance in teaching, learning, and research.

Historical Background

The evolution of higher education in India has been characterised by a gradual progression from traditional pedagogical models to an increasingly digitized learning environment. The inception of ICT in education can be traced back to the early 1990s when initiatives such as the National Mission on Education through Information and Communication Technology (NMEICT) were launched to promote the use of technology in teaching and learning. Subsequent policies and programmes, such as the Rashtriya Uchchatar Shiksha Abhiyan (RUSA) and the Digital India campaign, further underscored the significance of ICT in higher education reform.

However, despite these endeavours, the integration of ICT remained fragmented and uneven across institutions, hindered by infrastructural limitations, pedagogical inertia, and digital divide disparities. Recognizing the need for a holistic overhaul, NEP 2020 emerged as a seminal document aimed at redefining the contours of higher education in the digital era. By advocating for the adoption of ICT-enabled pedagogies, blended learning modalities, and digital infrastructure development, NEP 2020 seeks to foster a culture of innovation, collaboration, and lifelong learning in higher education institutions. This historical trajectory sets the stage for a deeper exploration of NEP 2020's transformative agenda and its implications for leveraging ICT as a catalyst for educational excellence and inclusive growth.

Main Recommendations of National Education Policy (NEP), 2020, for Higher Education with reference to ICT

Following are the main recommendation of NEP, 2020, for higher education with reference to ICT:

(i) **National Education Technology Forum (NETF):** A National Educational Technology Forum was proposed as an independent and sovereign body to provide a virtual platform for the free exchange of ideas regarding the use of technology to improve teaching, learning, assessment, management, and administration for all educational institutions in the country. The NETF's goal will be to facilitate decision making on technology induction, deployment, and use by providing the most recent knowledge and research to leaders of educational institutions, state and federal governments, and other stakeholders, as well as the opportunity to consult and share best practices.

(ii) **Pilot studies for online education:** Various agencies, including National Educational Technology Forum (NETF), Central Institute of Educational Technology (CIET), National Institute of Open Schooling (NIOS), Indira Gandhi National Open University (IGNOU), Industrial Training Institute (IIT), and National Institute of Technology (NIT), will conduct pilot studies to assess the benefits of integrating online education while minimizing drawbacks. The studies will also explore related topics like student device addiction and preferred e-content formats. Pilot study findings will be shared with the public and used to drive continuous improvement.

(iii) **Blended models of learning:** While promoting digital learning and education, the importance of face-to-face in-person learning is completely recognized. Covid-19 teaching, as a result, various effective blended learning models will be identified for appropriate replication across different subjects.

(iv) **Online assessment and examination:** Assessment frameworks will be designed and implemented by appropriate bodies, including the proposed National Assessment Centre or Performance Assessment, Review and Analysis of Knowledge for Holistic Development (PARAKH), School Boards, National Testing Agency (NTA), and others. These frameworks will include competencies, portfolios, rubrics, standardized assessments, and analytics. Studies will be conducted to test new methods of assessment using educational technologies that focus on 21st century skills.

(v) **Academic Bank of Credit:** The Academic Bank of Credit introduced in the NEP, 2020, aims to promote flexibility, mobility, and inclusivity in the higher education system by facilitating the recognition and transfer of academic credits, thereby empowering students to pursue diverse learning pathways and achieve their educational aspirations.

(vi) **Online teaching platform and tools:** Existing e-learning platforms, such as Study Webs of Active learning For Young aspiring Minds (SWAYAM) and Digital infrastructure for Knowledge Sharing (DIKSHA), will be expanded to offer teachers a structured and user-friendly set of tools to track learners' progress. The current pandemic has demonstrated the importance of tools such as two-way video and two-way audio interfaces for holding online classes.

(vii) **Virtual labs:** Existing e-learning platforms such as DIKSHA, SWAYAM, and SWAYAMPRABHA will also be used to create virtual labs, ensuring that all students have equal access to high-quality practical and hands-on experiment-based learning opportunities. The possibility of providing adequate access to Socio-Economically Disadvantaged Group (SEDG) students and teachers via suitable digital devices, such as tablets with pre-loaded content, will be considered and explored.

(viii) **Digital infrastructure:** To address India's scale, diversity, complexity, and device penetration, investments should be made in the development of open, interoperable, evolvable, public digital infrastructure in the education sector that can be used by multiple platforms and point solutions. This will ensure that technology-based solutions remain relevant in the face of rapid technological advancement.

(ix) **Lays down standard:** Setting standards: As research on online/digital education emerges, NETF and other appropriate bodies will establish standards for content, technology, and pedagogy for online/digital teaching-learning. These standards will assist states, boards of education, schools and school complexes, higher education institutions, and others in developing e-learning guidelines.

(x) **Addressing the digital divide:** To address the digital divide, existing mass media platforms like television, radio, and community radio will be utilised for broadcasts. To meet the diverse needs of the student population, such educational programmes will be available 24 hours a day, seven days a week in multiple languages etc. A special emphasis will be placed on content in all Indian languages; digital content must be delivered to teachers and students in their preferred medium of instruction.

Conclusion

The National Education Policy (NEP) 2020 is a significant step towards the transformation of higher education in India, focusing on the integration of Information and Communication Technology (ICT). The policy aims to democratise access to education by promoting online and blended learning models, breaking down geographical and socio-economic barriers, and making quality education more accessible to learners across the country. This democratisation not only expands educational opportunities for marginalised communities but also fosters greater inclusivity and diversity within the higher education ecosystem. The policy also emphasizes the importance of digital literacy and technological fluency in the 21st-century workforce. By integrating ICT across curricula and pedagogical practices, the policy aims to equip learners with the necessary skills and competencies to thrive in an increasingly digital and interconnected world. Through hands-on exposure to emerging technologies, students are empowered to adapt to rapidly evolving job markets and contribute to innovation and economic growth. The policy also recognizes the catalytic role of ICT in enhancing the quality and relevance of higher education. By fostering collaborations between academia, industry, and research institutions, the policy aims to harness the power of technology-enabled innovation in curriculum design, pedagogy, and assessment. The NEP 2020 envisions the creation of a robust digital infrastructure and ecosystem to support the seamless integration of ICT in higher education. By embracing technology as a catalyst for innovation, inclusion, and excellence, the policy sets a bold vision for the future of higher education, characterised by flexibility, accessibility, and relevance in the digital age.

References

Amirullah, "National education policy-2020 in Open and Distance Learning Through ICT." *International Journal of Multidisciplinary Educational Research*, vol. 5, no. 6, 2023, http://s3-ap-southeast-1.amazonaws.com/ijmer/pdf/volume11/volume11-issue12(5)/4.pdf.

Barla, Pushpalata and Awadh Kishor Trivedi, " A Study on the Impact of ICT in Higher Education with Special Reference to NEP 2020." *Journal of Emerging Technologies and Innovation Research (JETIR),* Vol. 10, no. 8, 2023, https://www.jetir.org/papers/JETIR2308501.pdf.

Bhat, Khurshid Ahmad and Zahida Ashraf, "National education Policy 2020: An Academic intuitive Into the Reforms It will Incorporate in School and Higher Education of India." *International Journal of Advanced Multidisciplinary Research,* Vol. 10, no. 2, 2023, pp. 22-28, ijarm3.pdf .

Kumari, Deepa, "New Education Policy 2020 Paradigm Shift in Education." *International Journal of Science and Research (IJSR)*, vol. 11, no. 6, 2022, New Education Policy 2020 Paradigm Shift in Education (ijsr.net).

Muralidharan, Kunnummal., Kulandaivel Shanmugan and Yury Klochkov, "The New Education Policy 2022, Digitalisation and Quality of Life in India: Some reflections." *Education Sciences*, vol. 12, no. 25, 2022, https://files.eric.ed.gov/fulltext/EJ1340481.pdf.

"National Education Policy 2020" Ministry of Education, n.d., https://www.education.gov.in/sites/upload_files/mhrd/files/NEP_Final_English_0.pdf.

Nandy, Sunipa Sammadder, "National education policy-2020: A digital initiative to integrate ICT in higher education." *International Journal of Applied Research*, Vol. 8, no. 5, 2022, National education policy-2020: A digital initiative to integrate ICT in higher education (allresearchjournal.com).

Sawant, Rupesh G. and Umesh B. Sankpal, "National education Policy 2020 and Higher Education: A Brief Review." *International Journal of Creative research Thoughts (IJCRT)*, Vol. 9. No. 1, 2021, pp. 3456-3460, https://www.ijcrt.org/papers/IJCRT2101423.pdf.

Sharma, Panchali, "A Paradigm Shift in Education: Understanding the NEP 2020." *International Journal of Innovations & Research Analysis (IJIRA)*, Vol. 3, no. 2(II), International-Journal-of-Innovations-Research-Analysis-IJIRA-Vol-3-No-2I-April-June-2023-Pages-01-to-08 (1).pdf.

Upadhyay, Ami, "Open and Distance Learning for Meeting Access Challenges in Implementation of National Education Policy." *National education policy-2020: Transforming Higher Education in India*, vol. 19, 2021, https://www.aiu.ac.in/documents/AIU_Publications/Wednesday_Essay/12.OPEN%20AND%20DISTANCE%20LEARNING%20FOR%20MEETING%20ACCESS%20CHALLENGES%20IN%20IMPLEMENTATION%20OF%20NATIONAL%20EDUCATION%20POLICY%E2%80%932020%20By%20AMI%20Updadhyay,%20VC%20BAOU,%20Gujarat_07%20July%2021.pdf.

Chapter - 3

New Education Policy 2020: A Comparative Analysis with Existing National Policy of Education 1986

– Poonam Subedi & Dr. Sushant Kumar Nayak

Abstract

New Education Policy 2020 to shift the paradigm in the Indian education system to emphasizes Quality, Affordability, Equality, Access and Accountability which include more holistic approach, encouraging critical thinking, creativity and practical skills to better prepare students for the evolving demands of the modern world. The NPE 2020 was approved by the Union Cabinet of India on 29 July, 2020. The Ministry of Human Resource Development formed a committee headed by former ISRO Chairman Dr. Kasturiranjan, who outlined the vision of India's new education system. This is the 1st education policy of the 21st century and it replace the thirty-four old National Policy on Education, 1986. The main purpose of comparing the old education policy (NPE 1986) with the new education policy (NEP 2020) is to have a better understanding of the similarities and the differences of both the education policies. The main purpose of comparing the old education policy (NPE 1986) with the new education policy (NEP 2020). An attempt had been also made to figure out the changes and challenges in the existing policy that led to the emergence of NEP 2020. The data has been collected through various sources i.e., journals, reports, print media and various other government websites. This article is purely based on secondary data. Though NEP 2020 has new targets to be achieved by 2035, nevertheless it has its own merits and limitations and the efforts have been made to highlight them.

Keywords: New Education Policy 2020, National Policy of Education 1986, Comparison.

Introduction

Education is a key component in shaping the personality of an individual and governs his overall development. If we go by Ancient Indian thinkers, Education is like the 'third eye' of a person and gives him an insight into the significance and purpose of life. Thus, enabling him to act justly and rightly. Education structures and systems across the globe are facing paradigm change the recent trends emerging in the education scenario demand changes in educational policy and its governance framework, Secularism etc. For further progress in the education system, the Government of India should formulate a national policy for education in all economic classes and inclusion of common people. In 1968 Prime Minister Indira Gandhi proposed the first National Policy on Education by the Government of India. The second policy was NPE 1986 by Prime Minister Rajiv Gandhi and the third utmost reformative policy was in 2020 by Prime Minister Narendra Modi. National policy on education 1986 is mainly focused on access, enrollment and retention of all children up to the age of 14 years, a common education structure for all citizens; therefore equalisation of educational opportunities is the main features of NPE 1986. On the other hand the National Education Policy 2020 is based on Access, Quality, Equity and Affordability and Accountability. NEP 2020 emphasizes systematic, flexible, multidisciplinary academies and research mainly in higher education institutions in India. NEP 2020 emphasis systematic and institutional improvements to regulate govern and promote multidisciplinary academic and research in Indian HEIs. NEP 2020 has marked an epoch development in the educational landscape of India. The policy envisions an Indian centred education system compatible to transform India to a vibrant knowledge society. Remarkably, the thrust area of the new education policy is to make the system of education well-resourced and multidisciplinary by the consolidation of multiple educational institutions and disciplines which constantly strives to deliver the needs.

Reservation Methodology

The article is based on secondary data collected from various journals, newspapers and websites. The methodology consists of a conceptual discussion on the highlights of the NEP 2020 and the focus of this article is on the comparison of NEP 2020 with the current educational policy of India.

NPE 1986 – Overview

In 1985, the Government of India conducted a thorough examination of the existing education system, culminating in the document "Challenge of Education: A Policy Perspective." The visionary National Policy on Education, launched by former Prime Minister Rajiv Gandhi in May 1986, aimed to equip India for the challenges of the 21st century. Some of the significant highlights of NPE 1986 are as follows:

- 10 + 2 + 3 structure of Education.
- Early childhood care and Education
- Child centered and activity-centered teaching methodology,
- Equal opportunity for all.
- Minimum levels of learning for each stage of education.
- Life-long education.
- Education for Equality
- Removal of women's illiteracy.
- Education of minorities.
- Education of the handicapped.
- Universal enrolment and universal retention of children upto 14 years of age
- Child – Centered Approach
- Pace setting schools for talented children, largely rural.
- Technical and Management Education.
- Emphasizes mother tongue as the medium of instruction at the primary level

Limitations of the Policy

- Neglecting the 'Neighbourhood school' concept: The

concept of 'Neighbourhood school' given by Kothari Commission (1964-66) has been completely ignored. Kothari Commission recommended this concept to lessen the differences between the rich and poor.

- Multiplication of authorities: The multiplicity of authorities in education has been recommended. Role of various authorities have not been properly defined.
- No place for Basic Education: The National Policy on Education has no place for basic education, besides in the struggle of independence it had played an important role.
- Silence over the existence of Public schools and their commercialisation.
- Financial implications of the implementation of educational reforms have not been worked out.
- Too much expectations from community help.

New Education Policy 2020

This is the first education policy of the 21st century and will replace the thirty-four-year-old National Policy on Education (NPE), 1986.This policy was passed after more than three decades. New education policy 2020 has comprehensive overall vision and plays a central role in the Nation's future growth. NEP 2020 aims to increase the gross enrollment ration in higher education to 50 percentages by 2035. This policy introduces large multi-disciplinary University, College and higher educational institutions to end the fragmentation of Higher Education. Where aimed to 3000 or more students enrolled in a time. Also encouraging multi-disciplinary subjects in our education to provide students with a brother and more holistic understanding of various subjects. This policy executes of a credit transfer system to enable student to shift easily between institutions and programme and also allowing curriculum flexibility designed to fit student interest and career paths. Policy focused on promoting research and innovation in university and colleges to foster a culture of creativity and problem solving. And also encouraging internationalisation of higher education to foster global collaboration and exposure for students are faculty. Academic Bank of Credit is one of the key components introduced under NEP 2020 in India. The Academic Bank of Credit will serve as a digital repository of academic credits earned by students from various higher education institutions. This allow students to accumulate credits at once regardless of where they are earned. NEP 2020 also encourages a multiple entry and exit system, meaning that student can join and leave higher education programmes at different stages while still obtaining recognised qualifications. For higher education NEP offered 1 year diploma, 2-year Advance diploma, 3 year Graduation, 4 year Graduation with research. In NEP 2020 offers 1 year or 2 year master's degree after graduation. 1 year master's degree for those who have completed 4 year graduation and 2 year master degree for those who have completed 3 year graduation course. NEP 2020 proposed Higher Education Commission of India (HECI) a single wide umbrella regulatory body for entire higher education, except medical and legal education. It is aims to bring about reforms in the field of higher education and promote autonomy, innovation, and quality improvement in universities and colleges.

Comparison between NEP 2020 & NPE 1986

- NEP 2020 which was started by the Union Cabinet of India on 29 July 2020, outlines the vision of the new education system of India. But NPE 1986 was formulated by govt. of India to promote and regulate education in India
- NEP 2020 targets 50% GER in school education in the next 10 years and also envisions universalisation of education from pre-school to secondary level. But NPE 1986 targets 26.3% in higher education on 2018
- NEP 2020 declared a 5+3+3+4 structure which has a strong base of Early Childhood Care and Education (ECCE) from age 3 is included, which is aimed at promoting better overall learning, development, and well-being. But NPE 1986 declared a 10+2+3 structure which made that the primary stage should consist of 5 years and 3 years of upper primary

followed by 2 years of high school, efforts will also be made to have the +2-stage accepted as a part of school education throughout the country.

- NEP 2020 announced 4 stages like- Foundational stage (Ages 3 to 8 years), Preparatory stage (Ages 8 to 11 years), Middle Stage (Ages 11 to 14 years) & Secondary stage (Ages 14 to 18 years). But NPE 1986 envisages a common educational structure where the first 10 years followed school education, the next 2 years followed higher secondary education and next 3 years followed university education.
- NEP 2020 recommended 3 language formulas, first- Mother tongue or regional language, second- in Hindi-speaking states, it will be other modern Indian languages or English, third in Hindi-speaking states, it will be English or a modern Indian language. But NPE 1986 states 3 Language formula that schools must teach Hindi, English, and One modern Indian Language.
- NEP 2020 declared there will be no rigid separation between Arts and Science streams and curricular and extra-curricular activities in school education and higher education, it will now follow a multi- disciplinary approach. But NPE 1986 announced a hard separation between Art, Science & Commerce.
- NEP 2020 announced the board exam will be made 'easier', class 10 and 12 board exams will test primarily core capacities, and competencies rather than memorisation. But the NPE 1986 board exam is based on memorizing and adapting to continuous evaluation and grading system.
- NEP 2020 declared School education would be 12 years of schooling with 3 years of Anganwadi. But NPE 1986 announced an Elementary system.
- Comprising 5 years of primary and 3 years of upper – primary and 2 years of high school education.
- NEP 2020 redesigned report cards will be a holistic, 360-degree, multidimensional report that reflects in great

detail the progress and the uniqueness of each learner in cognitive, affective, and psychomotor domains. The progress report will include self- assessment, peer assessment, and teacher assessment. But in NPE 1986, report cards were only reviewed by teachers.

- NEP 2020 has set the target to increase public investment in the education sector to reach 6% of the Gross Domestic Product (GDP) at the earliest. But NPE 1986 declared education sector gets 4.5% of the GDP.
- NEP 2020 emphasized the usage of technology in education. E-content will be developed in eight regional languages Tamil, Telegu, Kannada, Malayalam, Gujarati, Marathi, Bengali, and Oriya. But NPE 1986 Integration of computer-education modules in professional and general education courses at the first-degree level and provision of computer facilities in these institutions initiated in the 7th Plan to be completed by 1995.
- NEP 2020 says, Not more than 30 students in a -class. Areas having large numbers of socio- economically disadvantaged students will aim for a PTR of under 25:1. But NPE 1986 declared at the primary level the PTR should be 30:1 but upper primary level it should be 35:1.
- NEP 2020 announced that National Testing Agency (NTA) will conduct one common entrance exam for admissions to all the universities and colleges for undergraduate degrees. But NPE 1986 to formulate a national examination reform work the Department of Education would, inter-alia, constitute an inter-institutional Committee with representations from UGC, NCERT, AICTE, and state-level organisations including the Board of Secondary Education.
- NEP 2020 declared ABC is a virtual storehouse that contains information on the credits earned by individual students throughout their learning journey, it will enable students to open their accounts and give multiple options for entering

and leaving colleges or universities. But the NPE 1986 does not say about credit scoring.

- The NEP 2020 calls for key reforms in both school and higher education that prepare the next generation to thrive and compete in the new digital age. Thus, there is much emphasis on multidisciplinary, digital literacy, written communication, problem-solving, logical reasoning, and vocational exposure in the document. But the NPE 1986 recommends that the institutions of national importance like UGC, NCERT, NIEPA, AICTE, ICAR, IMC, etc. will be strengthened to enable them to give shape to the national system of education and to cope with the emerging demands of the nation.
- NEP 2020 declared The MPhil programme is discontinued for the more research-oriented undergraduate and master's degrees and also said A doctorate can be pursued after a Master's. But NPE 1986 recommendations MPhil is a short-term research degree for students, which provides them exposure to research work and more options for advanced academic work.
- NEP 2020 announced controlling authorities like- HECI, NHERC, GEC, HEGC, and NAC. But NEP- 1986 declared about controlling authorities like- UGC, ICAR, BCI, CCIM, CBSE, and NCERT.
- NEP 2020 has recommended taking up five components of Adult Education- (a) foundational literacy and numeracy (b) critical life skills (c) vocational skills development (d) basic education (including preparatory, middle, and secondary stage equivalency); and continuing education (including engaging holistic adult education courses in arts, sciences, technology, culture, sports). But NPE 1986 declared Adult education to be the application of science & technology and pedagogical research for improving the pace and environment of learning and Establishing a linkage between adult education and the developmental programmes.

- The NEP 2020 stated that there will be 'no hard – separation' between the 'vocational and academical streams'. Universal access to all children of the = country to quality holistic education including vocational education – from preschool to Grade XII will be ensured while allowing for flexibility and choice of subjects. A National Committee for = Integration of Vocational Education (NCIVE) consisting of experts in vocational education and representatives from across Ministries, in collaboration with industry, will oversee the efforts of the implementation of VET. But NPE 1986 said about Vocational Education at the primary stage of education from class 1 to 5 Socially Useful Productive Work (SUPW) and at the higher secondary stage are to be regarded not as a preparation for college, but as a period for preparing an increasingly large number of school-leavers for different vocations in life.
- The National Education Policy 2020 (NEP 2020) aims to devise four National Curriculum Frameworks (NCFs), for which a comprehensive strategy has been worked out jointly by the Ministry of Education (MoE) and the National Council of Educational Research and Training (NCERT). But NPE-1986 emphasized early childhood education, strategies that involved total development of the child, i.e. physical, motor, cognitive, language, emotional, social, and moral, essential for children below the age of 6 years.
- In NEP 2020, The Government directly takes an active initiative in creating an integrated B.Ed. the programme takes four academic years to complete. National Council for Teacher Education (NCTE) supervises teacher training in this regard and promotes B.A. – B.Ed. a scheme that helps future – teachers achieve their maximum potential. NPE 1986 Declared The existing programme for teacher educators will be suitably modified considering the present-day training needs. The induction and continuing training programmes for the DIETs/CTEs/SCERTs faculty will be designed and implemented by the NCERT, NIEPA.

Advantages

- The Government aims to make schooling available to everyone with the help of NEP 2020.
- Approximately two crore school students will be able to come back to educational institutes through this new approach.
- According to the national education policy 2020, the 5+3+3+4 structure will replace the existing 10+2 structure. This structure is focused on student's formative years of learning. This 5+3+3+4 structure corresponds to ages from 3 to 8, 8 to 11, 11 to 14 and 14 to 18. 12 years of schooling, 3 years if Anganwadi and pre-schooling are included in this structure.
- For children up to the age of 8, a National Curricular and Pedagogical Framework for Early Childhood Care and Education will be designed and developed by NCERT.
- According to the national education policy 2020, the Education Ministry is to set up a National Mission on Foundational Literacy and Numeracy. The responsibility for successful implementation for achieving the foundation of numeracy and literacy for all students till class three falls upon the states of India. This implementation is scheduled to be done by 2025.
- One of the merits of NEP 2020 is the formation of the National Book promotion Policy in India.
- Appropriate authorities will conduct the school examinations for grades 3, 5 and 8. The board exams for grades 10 and 12 will continue but the NEP 2020 aims to re-design the structure with holistic development.
- Parakh national education policy is to be set up by the Government.
- Special daytime boarding school "Bal Bhavans" to be established in every state/ district in India. This boarding school will be used for participation in activities related to play, career, art.

- According to the national education policy 2020, an Academic Bank of Credit will be established. The credits earned by the students can be stored and when the final degree gets completed, those can be counted.
- According to the national education policy 2020, Multi-disciplinary Education and Research Universities at par with the IITs and IIMs will be set up in the country. These are scheduled to be set up for introducing multidisciplinary academic.
- The same list of accreditation and regulation rules will be used for guiding both the public and private academic bodies.
- Phased out college affiliation and autonomy will be granted to colleges.
- By the year 2030, it will be mandatory to have at least a four year B. Ed degree for joining the occupation of teaching.
- For making the students prepared for future pandemic situations, online academic will be promoted on a larger scale.

Drawbacks

1. In the National Education Policy 2020, language is a negative factor as there is a problematic teacher to student ratio in India, thus introducing mother languages for each subject in academic institutes is a problem. Sometimes, finding a competent teacher becomes a problem and now another challenge comes with the introduction of the NEP 2020, which is bringing study material in mother languages.
2. According to the national education policy 2020, students willing to complete their graduation have to study for four years while one can easily complete his/ her diploma degree in two years. This might encourage the pupil to leave the course midway.
3. According to the national education policy 2020, students of the private schools will be introduced to English at a much

earlier age than the students of the Government schools. The academic syllabus will be taught in the respective regional languages of the Government school students. This is one of the major new education policy drawbacks as this will increase the number of students uncomfortable in communicating in English thus widening the gap between sections of the societies.

Conclusion

It is concluded that the Indian government has formulated educational policies regularly to ensure that the Indian education system is of high quality and internationally recognized. The two previous national educational policies have helped to develop India's educational system, and the action plan for the third national educational policy is one of the platforms that will be used. The policy's results will be evaluated using the outcomes of the current national education policy's action plan. If this policy focuses on the root causes of the issues and difficulties it faces, it will be effective It.

References

Babu, Dr. M. Ravi, "NEP 2020: Issues and Challenges Ahead in Teacher Education." *The International Journal of Indian Psychology,* Vol. 11, no. 3, Sept. 2023, https://doi.org/DOI: 10.25215/1103.424.

Choudhari, Dr. Deepa, "A Study on National Education Policy – 2020 and Its Impact on Stakeholders w.r.t Higher Education Institutions of Nagpur City." *International Journal of Research Publication and Reviews,* vol.3, no. 2, Feb. 2022, https://ijrpr.com/uploads/V3ISSUE2/ijrpr2644-a-study-on-national-education-policy2020.pdf

G. Sawant, Dr. Rupesh, and Dr. Umesh B. Sankpal, "National Education policy 2020 and Higher Education: A Brief Review." *International Journal of Creative Research Thoughts* (Vol. 9, no. 1, Jan. 2021.

Kurien, Ajay, Impact of New Education Policy 2020 on Higher Education. 2020, https://doi.org/DOI:10.6084/m9.figshare.13332413.v1.

Lukose, Merin, and Pankhuri Sharma, "A Study on the Role of NEP 2020: Skill Development of Students ." *Amity International Journal of Teacher Education* (Vol. 9, no. 1, Apr. 2023.

Mandal, Md Abdul Aziz, "A Critical Analysis of the National Education Policy 2020: Implications and Challenges." *International Journal of Research*

Publication and Reviews, Vol. 4, no. 7, July 2023, https://ijrpr.com/uploads/V4ISSUE7/IJRPR15493.pdf.

MR, Shubhada, and MR, Niranth, "NEW EDUCATION POLICY 2020: A COMPARATIVE ANALYSIS WITH EXISTING NATIONAL POLICY OF EDUCATION 1986." International Journal of Research and Analytical Reviews (IJRAR) © 2021 IJRAR May 2021, Volume 8, Issue 2, May. 2020, https://risingkashmir.com/enshrined-in-nep-2020-what-does-rootedness-in-india-means#:~:text=The%20New%20Education%20Policy%20of,and%20culturally%20rich%20educational%20experience

Rani, Dr. Ruchi, "National Education Policy-2020: Issues and Challenges." *Journal of Research in Humanities and Social Science,* Vol. 10, no. 2.

Rayees, Ahmad. Changing Role of Teacher Educators in View of NEP 2020. Jan. 2023, https://doi.org/DOI:10.31426/ijamsr.2021.4.11.4911566662345.

Singh, Kaurav, Dr, Rahul Pratap, et al., "New education policy: qualitative (contents) analysis and twitter mining (sentiment analysis)." Journal of Content, Community & Communication, Vol. 12, no. 6, Dec. 2020.

Verma, Dr. Hemlata, and Adarsh Kumar, "New Education Policy 2020 of India: A Theoretical Analysis." International Journal of Business and Management Research, Vol. 9, no. 3, Aug. 2021, https://doi.org/DOI:10.37391/IJBMR.090308.

Chapter - 4

The National Education Policy 2020: Transformation, Issues And Challenges

– Dr. Neena Hamid & Bijaya Das

Abstract

The National Education Policy 2020 (NEP-2020) is embarked upon a vision of transforming the system to meet the needs of 21st century India. Education policies worldwide are increasingly being realigned to economic prosperity, vertical mobility, and social citizenship of the people. One of the fundamental principles of the NEP 2020 is "flexibility so that learners can choose their learning trajectories and programmes, and thereby choose their paths in life according to their talents and interests". Here, the NEP 2020 shows us the way, as It recommends an interdisciplinary structure of programmes. Integrative thinking is the need of the hour and our education policymakers may very well start with themselves in this journey. There is an urgent need to re-examine our education policies at the regional level to provide an environment where individuals can utilise their education and training to gain employment, improve their living standards, and contribute to the social development of the area. The paper suggested some measures to preserve quality education and promote the transformation of educators towards the changing nature of work.

Key Words: Flexibility, Transformation, Interdisciplinary, Mobility.

Introduction

With the introduction of the National Education Policy 2020 (NEP), a new era of transformation has begun. NEP has emerged as a game-changer, promising to bridge the educational divide and empower students in remote areas. The primary objective is to bridge the gap between rural and urban areas by emphasizing access, equity, quality, affordability, and accountability. It gives utmost priority to recognising, identifying, and fostering unique capabilities to promote each student's holistic development. So, the goal is to nurture talent through critical thinking and problem-solving, and a strong emphasis on a more practical, hands-on, creative, and skill-based approach is the priority.

The policy also envisages a wider and more intensive role for the use of technology for the purposes of improving teaching-learning and evaluation processes, teachers' professional development, enhancing educational access, streamlining educational planning, management, and administration, including processes related to admissions, attendance, assessments, etc. The role of education will also be to assist in raising awareness about the potential disruptive effects of technology and to address related issues.

Further, the recent pandemic compelled us to be prepared with alternative modes of quality education, and blended learning is the future of the 21st century. The benefits of the availability of online education and existing digital platforms need to be optimised and expanded further to meet the current and future challenges of improving quality education for all. In this regard, it has become all the more relevant to invest in public digital infrastructure in the education sector that multiple stakeholders can use, keeping in view India's large-scale diversity, complexity, and device penetration.

Historical Development

The first National Education Policy in 1968 was formed during the time of the Indira Gandhi Government. The second National Education Policy was 1986 was formed during the Rajiv Gandhi Govt. It was modified in 1992 by P.V. Narsimha Rao Govt. Now after 34 years, the new National Education Policy 2020 (NEP 2020) is coming to society. In the new Central Government of 2014, a new committee was formed on New Education Policy in 2015 under the chairmanship of T.S.R. Subramanian. The Report was submitted on 7th May 2016. The main objectives of the committee include - (i) To improve the quality of the Education, (ii) Credibility of Education, (iii) Addressing the gaps in implementation. Another New committee was formed and made up of members and they drafted the National Education Policy in 2019 under the chairmanship of Dr. Krishnaswamy Kasturirangan.

(a) National Policy on Education, 1986

Historically, since independence, various education policies have emphasized equality in education. Particularly, the National Policy on Education (NEP) 1986/1992 laid special emphasis on the removal of disparities. Education should be used as an agent of basic change in the status of women. It was envisaged that the policy would neutralise the accumulated distortions of the past through a well-conceived edge in favour of women. It would foster the development of new values through redesigned curricula, and textbooks, the training and orientation of teachers, decision-makers and administrators and the active involvement of educational institutions. The removal of women's illiteracy and obstacles inhibiting their access to, and retention, in elementary education will receive overriding priority, through the provision of special support services, setting of time targets and effective monitoring. The policy of non-discrimination will be pursued vigorously to eliminate sex stereotyping in vocational and professional courses and to promote women's participation in non-traditional occupations, as well as in existing and emergent technologies. Following the policy directives of NPE, several States and National Education programmes like the Basic Education Programme, BEP, OBB, DPEP, SSA and RMSA. The Right to Children to Free and Compulsory Act, 2009 (RTE Act), was a key milestone for elementary education in the country.

(b) Challenges as per New Education Policy 2016

The inputs for NEP 2016 recognize that relatively higher

gender gaps in youth and adult literacy rates remain a principal challenge. India continues to be characterised by a higher level of gender gap (8.2 percentage points) in youth literacy rate, with the youth literacy rates for male and female populations (age 15-24) in 2011 being 90 percent and 81.8 percent respectively. India also continues to be the country with a higher level of gender gap (19.5 percentage points) in adult literacy. It is clear that major efforts are needed to raise the literacy levels of girls and women.

(c) National Education Policy 2020

The NEP 2020 is embarked upon a vision of "transforming the system to meet the needs of 21st century India." More than two decades ago, UNESCO published a ground-breaking report *Learning The Treasure Within for the International Commission on Education for the Twenty-first Century,* chaired by Jacques Delors. It argued for an integrated vision for education and learning worldwide, which influenced our educational policies for many years. With free market economic reforms and the socio-economic transformation of the societies post-1990s, it is relevant to revisit the report and revisit the educational policies adopted. One of the prominent recommendations for the education sector was to underline the concept of 'learning to be', which emphasizes an individual's autonomy to grow in a specific direction of inherent interest, call it a passion, and achieve one's dream in life. Our policymakers in the north-east region need to re-emphasize this point in coming years as it is also supported by the guidelines of NEP 2020. One of the fundamental principles of the NEP 2020 is "flexibility so that learners can choose their learning trajectories and programmes, and thereby choose their paths in life according to their talents and interests." Here the NEP 2020 shows the way as it recommends interdisciplinary structure of programmes.

Objectives

1. To understand the contribution of the New Education Policy 2020 to the social development of Indian citizens.
2. To preserve quality education and promote the transformation of integrative thinkers.
3. To examine the issues and the way forward that link Education Policies to the wider challenges of the region.

Methodology: The humble approach of this paper is a descriptive study based on secondary sources of data which are doctrinal in nature.

Initiatives undertaken by the Ministry of Education

Several initiatives have been undertaken by the Department of School Education and literacy towards nurturing the talent in rural India and strengthening the digital infrastructure and online learning facilities.

Nurturing the talent of students

The NEP 2020 aims to focus on the holistic development and critical thinking of students. It promotes experiential learning, creativity, and problem-solving skills, enabling all students to develop a well-rounded personality, initiatives are given below:

- **Pradhan Mantri Innovative Learning Programme-Dhruv** has been started to identify and encourage talented children to enrich their skills and knowledge, gifted children are mentored and nurtured by renowned experts in different areas, so that they can reach their full potential. In this regard, a detailed guideline is under process, which will be aligned with the recommendations of NEP 2020.
- **Samagra Shiksha:** The centrally sponsored scheme has various interventions, like the establishment of Youth club and Eco clubs to showcase their innate talents and hone their skills. Also, activities like Kala Utsav, Rangotsav, Ek Bharat Shreshtha Bharat, Band Competition, etc. are supported in

the schools, wherein children get an opportunity to exhibit their innate talent.

- **Ek Bharat Shreshtha Bharat (EBSB):** The programme was launched by the Hon'ble Prime Minister on Ekta Diwas (31st 2015) to foster integration through a coordinated mutual engagement process between States, UTs, Central Ministries, Educational Institutions, and the general public through linguistic, literary, cultural, sports, tourism, and other forms of people-to-people exchanges.

  The Ministry of Education issued revised guidelines on 20th November 2020 for the implementation of the EBSB programme in the States/UTs, and an illustrative list of suggested activities has been taken up in schools in accordance with NEP 2020. Till January 2022, 4 crore students participated in EBSB activities at the school level. In addition, 3.5 lakh EBSB clubs have been formed so far in KVS, NVS, CBSE, and other schools in the States and UTs. Bhasha Sangam, an initiative to promote multilingualism under EBSB, marks the unique symphony of languages in our country and is an expression of our shared dreams, hopes, and aspirations for one India. Under this, NCERT has developed 100 sentences in 22 Indian languages under Schedule VIII of the Constitution of India.

- **Navodaya Vidyalayas** selects students for residential schooling on the basis of an all-India competitive entrance exam. Its significance lies in the selection of talented rural children as the target group and the attempt to provide them with a 'quality education, comparable to the best in a residential school system. The identified talented children are nurtured and educated from class 6th to 12th grade in the Vidyalayas until they complete schooling.

  The National Talent Search Scheme (NTSE) of the National Council of Educational Research and Training (NCERT) identifies and nurtures students seized through a two-tier process every year. The school helps talented students by providing financial assistance in the form of monthly scholarships and also conducts nurturing programmes for them.

Most Important Changes in NEP 2020

The main objective of the new education policy 2020 is universalisation of education achieving global standards of education.

Most Important Changes in the new NEP 2020
1. The HRD Ministry is now reframed as the Ministry of Education.
2. GDP investment in Education to increase from 1.6/ to 6/.
3. Focusing on Gross Enrolment Ratio it will be increased to 50/ by 2035.
4. To foster research culture in Higher Education NATIONAL RESEARCH FOUNDATION will be set up as an apex body.
5. To improve the Multidisciplinary Education will establish MERU-MULTIDISCIPLINARY EDUCATION AND RESEARCH UNIVERSITIES.
6. For Higher Education HECI- HIGHER EDUCATION COMMISSION OF INDIA will be set up as a dedicated & soul body excluding Medical & Legal Education.
7. Single regulator for Higher Education (Excluding Medical & Legal).
8. MPhil to be discontinued.
9. Flexibility of subjects.
10. Public investment in Education to reach 6/ of GDP at the earliest.

Significance of Early Childhood

Early childhood is the period from birth to six years of age. There is enough evidence provided by research, which proves that early childhood is a very crucial phase of one's life. Starting from home, almost all families should really take care of their children during early childhood. We have made interventions in the natural development of human beings through education. Education is the all-round development of human beings. Therefore, it can be said that education is a developmental intervention. This intervention is delivered in three ways-formal, informal and non-formal. Out of these, informal education is more natural than formal and non-formal. In general, we have the tendency to believe that informal education is enough for the early childhood stage. But looking at the potential of this stage, we have a lot of opportunities to shape the natural development of the child in a socially desirable way. It would always be worthy to, at least try our best to provide adequate opportunities for development. It would be an injustice on the part of the child if it does not get adequate and appropriate opportunities for its optimum development. Unfortunately, this indeed is happening to a large population.

If we recall history, we find that early childhood education could draw the attention of the people, particularly the policy-makers very late and in fewer numbers. Just after independence, India rationally gave attention to higher education (University Education Commission, 1948-49) and secondary education (Secondary Education Commission, 1952-53). The first national policy on education which came up in 1968 recommended the structure of education in the National educational system as 10+2+3. It did not count early childhood education in the structure. After this, the national policy for children came up in 1974. This policy resulted in the Integrated Child Development Scheme (ICDS) under the department of social welfare. Early childhood education could gain a place in 1986 which recognised the need for holistic and integrated child development. It still is in isolation from the Department of Human Resource Development which is responsible for the educational development of the country. The ICDS takes care of both the pre-natal and early childhood stages.

A significant development towards early childhood education was the establishment of Anganwadis/Balvatika as a 'playground' for children of 3-6 years of age. The Anganwadi workers have the huge responsibility of taking care of not only the children of age group 3-6 years but also of those in the 0-3 years group, pregnant mothers, lactating mothers and adolescent girls. But in return, their salary/wage does not count what they are actually doing, not what they are actually doing on the ground. This, of course, is a situation to cause concern. The child will perform in the matriculation or in the higher secondary examination or in fact, in the later life on the basis of the developmental opportunities it receives during the early years. So, the best and substantial care that the parents need to take for the education of their children is their early years, and not during matriculation or higher secondary examination. Fortunately, the National Educational Policy 2020 has accepted the fact that over 85 percent of a child's cumulative brain development occurs prior to the age of 6. And it has also accepted the loophole that quality early childhood education is not available to a large population. It is gratifying to see that for the first time our national policy has emphasized universalisation of quality early childhood education by 2030. It is also good to see that early childhood education is able to secure its due place in the educational structure (5+3+3+4).

Table - 1

S. No.	**Comparative Analysis of Existing and Revised Academic Structure of NEP**		
1.	**Exiting Academic Structure**	• 10yrs- age-(10-16) • 2yrs- age-(16-18)	
	Pedagogical System		
2.	**Revised Academic Structure**	• 5yrs-(Anganwadi/Pre-school/ Balvatika) -Age(3-6) Class(1&2) Age(6-8)	Formal Education as per Global Standards
		• 3yrs-Class (3-5) Age (8-11)	
		• 3yrs-Class (6-8) Age (11-14)	
		• 4yrs-Class (9-12) Age (14-18)	

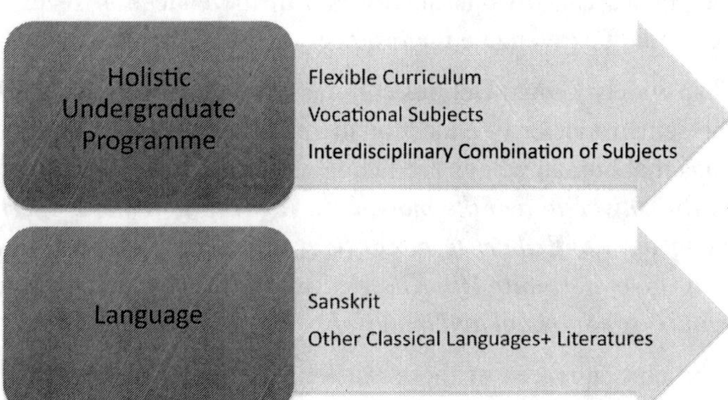

Visionary Approach of NEP 2020

Let education accept the challenge to assist in creating an environment for the individualised action plan that aims to transform every person into a personality. It is only possible by inculcating various innovative practices of value education as well as correlation of subjects. We need holistic education for our present and future generation because society needs creativity, problem-solving capacities, co-operation, cultural and moral sensitivity, care and craftsmanship. In order to enhance the self-esteem of all young people and provide optimal living conditions to all, we need this type of education which is concerned with both individual freedom and social responsibility for the development of humanity's inherent morality and spirituality in our educational system.

The pandemic has emphasized the importance and need for online education, due to which, a hybrid model of teaching, which involves offline as well as online classes, has now become a new trend in India. Considering the present scenario and the need for time, the university grants commission (UGC) has also recommended the application of modern teaching techniques, which include hybrid mode. Moreover, AI has also started playing an important role in the education system of India, the adoption of which needs to be further expanded. New Education Policy (NEP) has also been drafted and implemented incorporating all modes of teaching. It is realised that AI techniques can fill this quality gap in the education sector and hence should be given due importance.

The widely known Delores commission report (UNESCO,1996) that presented a vision of education in the 21st century identified seven tensions that human beings are facing at present: *(a) Global and the local, (b) Universal and the individual, (c) Tradition and modernity, (d) Long term and short term considerations, (e) Competition and equality of opportunity, (f) Knowledge explosion and capacity to assimilate, (g) Spiritual and material.*

The consequences of these tensions are now not only obvious to one and all on the planet earth, this calls for immediate corrective initiatives in several areas. All this leads to the visible presence of '*some sort of a moral crisis*' that every nation is facing at present.

A great visionary Mahatma Gandhi could see what would result in value erosion in future, if necessary, caution is not exercised by the systems of governance, and more importantly, by the people. In 1925, he published seven social sins in the *Young India* as *1. Commerce without morality, 2. Education without character, 3. Pleasure without conscience, 4. Politics without principles, 5. Science without humanity, 6. Wealth without work, 7. Worship without service.* These seven present the comprehensive guidelines for the planners and implementers of every country. India needs to acknowledge that unless it presents a model of value-based society in action, its dream of leading the world in spirituality shall remain a distant dream. Convert the above seven sins to Seven Individual Action Points; putting with instead of without; and witness the miracle!

We should keep in mind to define our policy objectives or strategic plan for the North East. Our students were dependent on 'permanent' government jobs for a long time, but these are now minuscule compared to a large number of 'educated' persons. The education systems, especially at the college and university level, are still focused around traditional subject areas granting degrees in specific domains. Hence, when an average student takes admission in any undergraduate programme, neither the student nor the educational administrators are ready with any plans to fit into a modern workplace in the coming years. The focus is on gaining a degree with knowledge in a specific domain that may be a very idealistic mission, but pragmatics demand that such a linear vision will not materialize if the need to 'get a job' in the near future. While keeping in mind that we need highly knowledgeable people and fundamental researchers to develop a subject area, there is also a practical necessity to think about a large number of students who will need some life skills or value-added training during these formative years to gain employment in a very competitive market. Our education policy restructuring for the region should start with this basic understanding.

Prof Srikant Datar, the globally acclaimed Indian-American economist and the dean of Harvard business school in his seminal co-authored work *"Rethinking the MBA: Business education at a crossroads,"* argues for a shift from 'knowing' to 'doing' and 'being' in education. Extending his argument to the education policymakers of the North East, we can say that our education systems need a similar rethinking whereby our governments, institutions, administrators and faculty should focus on restructuring our courses and programmes to incorporate three major elements – globalisation, leadership and integration.

1. **Globalisation** –

   The World Development Report 2019[5] makes three major recommendations that will feed into our 'globalisation' strategy for education. First, we need to focus on new skills in demand, invest in rural areas and disadvantaged communities, and include 'high-order cognitive and socio-behavioural components in our programmes. Developers of graduate and postgraduate programmes in the region should come together state-wise or even at the regional level, form inter-disciplinary groups and explore how courses, workshops and training components can be added to the mainstream curriculum to globalise them. By globalising, we mean to incorporate a set of understanding and training that will lead our students to understand the larger economic contexts of the country, demands of the market and trends of the global economy. In a narrower sense, students in a rural college in Mizoram or Tripura, while undertaking a course, should be familiarised with the prevalent working conditions, cultural nuances of other parts of the country and the world as part of their education.

2. **Leadership** –

   A re-orientation is necessary to include 'leadership skills' whereby our graduates are trained to develop a problem-solving approach, inter-cultural understanding to work with a diverse set of peers, and a sense of responsibility for their actions and influence on others. These qualities are not acquired in a day or just before a job interview. Specific courses should be introduced with motivational sessions mainstreaming across the programmes, and faculty-mentors should be assigned to guide them. Presently, it is left to individual students to acquire these skills outside of the programmes and often fail to impress a potential recruiter on these counts. Our universities and colleges need to launch 'leadership development' as a core component of all courses.

3. **Integration –**

   The third major redefining feature of our education policies in the region should include 'integration' skills in our education system. Our education programmes must offer training on acquiring a holistic approach to analyse any given issue from multiple perspectives involving other knowledge domains. Here the NEP2020 shows us the way as it recommends interdisciplinary structure of programmes. Today, students of political science should be able to join courses from computer science to look into social media politics. It will enhance their core learning in political theories and deal with the implications of technology in politics. We will need such professionals in the coming days with new jobs in domains like political campaigns or social media management. With a combination of statistics courses, the same graduates will be able to gain entry into the world of election result forecasting. Integrative thinking is the need of the hour, and our education policymakers may very well start with themselves in this journey.

Findings

An average educated youth in the North-East Region rarely has any clue about how he or she can utilise his knowledge and focus on entrepreneurship, professional career or even the job markets in the far east, especially with increased linkages with ASEAN countries.

The Indian constitution originally inserted education in the State List, and it was only during the Emergency and through the 42nd amendment to the Constitution that it was transferred to the Concurrent List. In actual practice though, it has almost become a subject of the Union List with the union government deciding and imposing its decisions on the architecture, funding and the actual operational guidelines on education from the primary to the higher levels. With the National Education Policy (NEP) 2020, this centralisation will move to newer heights.

As the NEP 2020 pledges to bring to an end the affiliating system, it will create enormous challenges for the existing public universities and also the universities to be established in the near future in conformity with the NEP 2020. The private universities will be benefited through the NEP 2020 due to their capacity to enhance fees, etc., to meet the requirements of the policy as well as for their commitment to drive as per the requirements of the market. Lowly paid teachers and officials in those universities will of course face the heat.

The NEP 2020 also provides a complete architectural shift in leadership and management of the universities. Under it the universities are all set to work in a corporate style with the VC's position becoming like that of a CEO of a company. The public universities will gradually be forced to go in for the public-private-partnership model, and in the long run, may result in the private partners taking over. There is already a crunch of avenues for critical thinking in the university system. Freedom of expression will be a rare thing in universities.

Policies have been made and implemented. But the situation does not seem to improve. The Anganwadi workers are the lowest paid teachers (if at all they are considered teachers) in the whole education system.

The infrastructural facilities of the Anganwadi centers are least taken care of. The professional development of elementary teachers is ensured through programmes like Diploma in Elementary Education

the right skills and mindset that the students from rural India can bring about transformative change in their communities, in the nation and globally. Our education system must facilitate such training as an integral part of the curriculum.

6. There is an urgent need to develop appropriate curriculum on entrepreneurship, contextualise the existing national skills qualifications framework (NSQF), curriculum for skilling at school level from grade 6 onwards and universalise digital skills training across all schools.
7. Without a trained set of counselors, course planners and mentors within the institutions, such a policy cannot be implemented. Therefore, we need to identify champions within our educators and administrators, reorient them towards the *changing nature of works* and convert them into mentors. Perhaps such a transformation is long overdue.

Addressing the students and teachers on the auspicious occasion of Teacher's Day, the Governor of Assam, Jagadish Mukhi said that National Education Policy, extensive changes have been made in the education system from school education to university level. With the cooperation and support of the people, the NEP is being fully implemented.

References

Article by Purabi Pattanayak, "Integrating Technology into Rural Education and Capacity Building of Teacher." Kurukshetra, November 2023, p. 33.

Article by Prof K M Baharul Islam, "*Educational Policy Interventions for the Region*", Yojana, July 2021, p. 34.

Article by Dr Krishna Kalita, "*Significance of early childhood*", The Assam Tribune, Date (15-06-22)

Article by Dr G P Dang, *et.al.*, *"AI in Education"*, Yojana, June, 2022, p. 27.

Article by Piyush Prakash, et.al., "*Changing Face of Rural Industries*", Kurukshetra, August, 2022, p. 9.

Article by Hemanth Menon, "*Rural Tourism-Culture and Heritage*", Kurukshetra, June, 2022, p.20.

Article by Padma Angmo, "*Education & Skilling"*, Yojana, September, 2022, p. 33.

Article by Dr Akhil Ranjan Dutta, *"Public Universities: Trapped in Multiple Crises"*, The Assam Tribune, Date (03-06-22).

Delors, J. (1996), "*Learning: the treasure within"*, Paris: UNESCO Publishing.

National Policy on Education 1986 (as modified in 1992).

Some inputs for draft NEP 2016, MHRD Supra Note 6, p. 32.

Srikant Datar, *et.al.*,(201), *Rethinking the MBA: Business Education at a Crossroads*. Boston: Harvard Business Press.

The Assam Tribune, 6th September, 2022.

World development report (2019): *The changing nature of work*, Washington DC, The World Bank.

World development report (2019): *The changing nature of work*, Washington DC, The World Bank.

Young India, October 22, 1925.

Yojana, September 2016, p. 58.

Chapter - 5

New Education Policy 2020 and Funding in Higher Education

– Oman Taloh

Abstract

In the development of an individual and the society as a whole, education has a very significant role to play. Education has the capacity to enlighten the soul of an individual and leads it to the light of freedom. Higher education has a significant role to play in the development of any nation. it has the capability to bring in positive socio-economic and moral changes in the society, it has been witnessed that though there have been tremendous increase in the quantity in the area of higher education, the qualitative growth have been somewhat dismal. Many problems are associated with the proper growth and development of higher education in india. She has her own issues that have to be tackled and challenges that has to be met in order to walk in the path of growth and development. National education policy is an attempt by the present Government to bring in positive changes in the existing educational system in India. The paper attempts to explain the trends of budgetary allocation in the higher education sector and to examine the challenges that is being faced in this sector.

Keywords: NEP 2020, higher education, funding trends, challenges.

Introduction

The socio-economic development of a country depends on the healthy higher education system. In the present era of knowledge driven economy, the role of higher education becomes instrumental in the overall socio-economic development of any region or country.

Institutions of higher education institutions contribute to the growth of a nation by providing specialised knowledge and skilled manpower (Alva Amitha, Dr Hans Basil, 2013). Higher education mainly focuses on teaching, research and extension. If we analyze the different concepts of higher education critically, then we can list the various roles higher education plays in the society. Higher education is the source or feeder system in all walks of life and therefore supplies the much-needed human resources management, planning, design, teaching and research. Scientific and technological advancement and economic growth of a country are also dependent on the higher education system. Development of indigenous technology and capabilities in agriculture, food security and other industrial areas are possible because of our world-class higher education. (Saranggi, Hota, 2018) After independence, India has witnessed a remarkable growth in the Higher Education system both in quantitative and qualitative terms. India's higher education system is the world's third largest in terms of students, next to China and the United States. Gross Enrollment ratio in India as per All India Survey on Higher Education (AISHE) 2019-20, the Gross Enrolment Ratio (GER) (enrolment in the population of the eligible age group) in higher education has increased from 25.8% in 2017-18 to 27.1% in 2019-20. However, it is still far from meeting the Ministry of Human Resource Development's target of achieving 32% GER by 2022. The National Education Policy (NEP) 2020 sets a target of achieving a 50% Gross Enrolment Ratio (GER) in higher education by 2035. This would require intensive institutional, infrastructural and policy changes to align with the mandates in NEP. Despite the increased access to higher education in India, challenges remain. Low employability of graduates, poor quality of teaching, weak governance, insufficient funding, and complex regulatory norms continue to plague the sector.

Objectives of this paper

1. to study the trend of budgetary allocation in higher educational Institutions (HEIs) and to inspect the change in funding pre and post NEP 2020.

2. to examine the trend of expenditure in higher education.
3. to make a comparative study with the developed countries.

Method of study

The study is based on secondary data collected from reputed articles of research journals, books, prominent sites relevant to higher education, magazines, etc. Second it is based on the experiences and observation of the author herself being a part of the higher education system and personal interview with the respondents.

The highlights of NEP-2020 for higher education section are listed below:

(1) Higher education (HE) monitoring and controlling institutions like UGC, AICTE, MCI, DCI, INC, etc will be merged with the Higher Education Commission of India (HECI) as a single regulator for HEIs.

(2) The current Accreditation Institutions such as NAAC and NAB will be replaced by a robust National Accreditation Council (NAC).

(3) Establishment of a National Research Foundation (NRF) to fund research in universities and colleges.

(4) Consolidation of existing fragmented HEIs into two types of Multidisciplinary Universities (MU) and Multidisciplinary Autonomous Colleges (AC) with the campus having more than 3,000 students.

The Timeline to become multi-disciplinary is by 2030 and have to be grown more than 3,000 students campus by 2040.

(5) Multidisciplinary Universities will be of two types as (1) Research-intensive Universities, and (2) Teaching -intensive Universities.

(6) Every existing College will develop into either degree granting autonomous College or migrated into a Constituent College of University and becomes fully a part of the University.

(7) The Gross Enrolment Ratio in HE, including Vocational education will be increased from the current 26.3% (2018) to 50% by 2035.

(8) HEIs, which deliver the highest quality will get more incentives from the government.

(9) All existing affiliated Colleges will eventually grow autonomous degree-granting colleges with the Mentoring support of affiliated universities by improving and securing the prescribed accreditation level.

(10) The nomenclature of HEIs in the country such as 'deemed to be university', 'affiliating university', 'affiliating technical university', 'unitary university' will be replaced simply by 'University' on fulfilling the criteria as per norms.

(11) Research will be included in UG, PG level, and have a holistic and multidisciplinary education approach.

(12) Pedagogy in HEIs will focus on an increased emphasis on communication, discussion, debate, research, and opportunities for cross-disciplinary and interdisciplinary thinking.

(13) An Academic Bank of Credit (ABC) will be established, which would digitally store the academic credits earned from various recognised HEIs (SWAYAM & ODL mode) so that the degrees from an HEI can be awarded taking into account credits earned.

(14) Four-year Bachelor's degree with multiple exit options, one to two-year Master's degree based on the number of years spent in Bachelor's degree as four or three, respectively, and option to do Ph.D. for four-year Bachelor's degree with research are possible.

(15) The post-graduate education will be reshaped with Two-year Master's degree with full research in the second year, One-year Master's degree for four-year Bachelor's degree holders, and Five-year integrated Bachelor's/Master's degree.

(16) All HEIs will focus on research and innovation by setting up (1) Start-up incubation centres, (2) Technology development

centres, (3) Centres in frontier areas of research, (4) Centre for Industry academic linkage, and (5) Interdisciplinary Research Centres including humanities and social science research.

(17) Student centred teaching and learning process will be implemented instead of current teacher centred teaching model.

(18) Choice Based Credit System is revised by an innovative and flexible Competency Based Credit System.

(19) Examination system will change from high-stakes examinations (Semester End system) towards a more continuous and comprehensive evaluation examination system.

(20) All HEIs will have professional academic and career counselling centres with counsellors available to all students to ensure physical, psychological, and emotional well-being.

(21) All HEIs will develop, support, and fund for topic-centred clubs and activities organised by students with the help of faculty and other experts as needed in the area of science, mathematics, poetry, language, literature, debate, music, sports, etc.

(22) Encouragement will be made for Online Distance Learning (ODL) courses as part of degree programmes to include the credit system.

(23) The Degree programmes may contain in-class teaching, Online teaching components, and ODL components with 40:30:30 ratio model to achieve a global standard of quality.

(24) HE quality will be improved to a global quality level to attract more international students and the credits acquired in foreign universities will be counted for the award of a degree.

(25) National Scholarship Portal will be strengthened and expanded to help the financial needs of meritbased students. Private HEIs will be encouraged to offer larger numbers of free ships and scholarships to their students.

Trends in Government spending on higher Education

Year	% of GDP
1990-91	0.43
1991-92	0.40
1992-93	0.38
1993-94	0.38
1994-95	0.37
1995-96	0.35
1996-97	0.33
1997-98	0.34
1998-99	0.37
1999-00	0.45
2000-01	0.46
2001-02	0.37
2002-03	0.38
2003-04	0.35
2004-05	0.32
2005-06	0.32
2006-07	0.32
2007-08	0.31
2008-09	0.37
2009-10	0.41

Source: Mitra A, 2015, public spending in higher education: a benefit incidence analysis+

In the Union Budget 2023-24, the higher education has received Rs 44,094 crore, an increase of 7.9 percent from Rs 40,828 crore in 2022-23. The further bifurcations of the budget focusing on,

Digital India e-learning has been allocated Rs 420 crore,

Research and innovation have been allocated Rs 210 crore which has increased 51 per cent over last year. The Scheme for Promotion of Academic and Research Collaboration (SPARC) which has been one of the funding sources for the Indian government to fund the UK-India Education Research Initiative programme gets a seven time increase from 10 crores to 74 crores.

University Grants Commission has been allocated Ra 5360 crore,

Indian Institute of Technology has been allocated Rs 9661 crore while Indian Institute of Management has been allocated Rs 300 crore,

When it comes to last year's Budget (2023-24), the allocation for the education and the higher education sector was just about 2.9 per cent of the country's GDP **(2.51**- primary+secondary+post secondary, **0.39**- Tertiary or Higher Education). Though small in absolute terms, it was still 8 per cent higher than the previous year. This trend of increasing spending on education is expected to continue this year as well.

However, if one compares the spending on education in other countries, the allocation is much less than the outlay by developed countries such as the United States (6 per cent of GDP) and the United Kingdom (4.2 of GDP). They meet the global expectations for budgetary allocation on education. Therefore, there is scope for India as well to increase its budgetary allocation in education from a mere 2.9 per cent of its GDP to 6 per cent.

Graph showing education expenditure as percentage of GDP and Total expenditure (2015-2022-23)

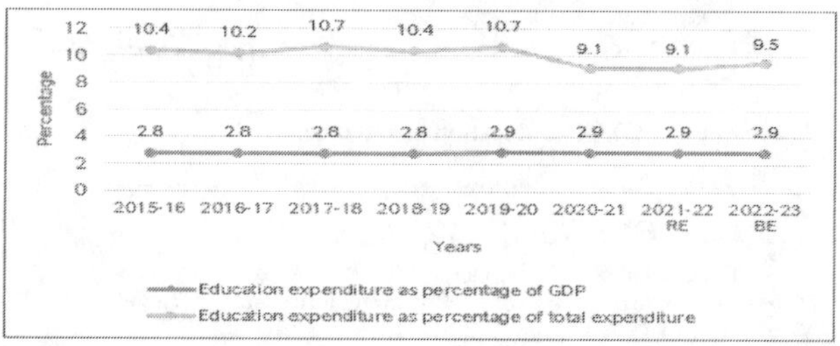

Source: Economic Survey 2022-23.

According to India's latest Economic Survey 2022-23, total education outlay, including both national and state level expenditure, added up to 2.9 per cent of the country's 2022 GDP – a proportion that has remained constant for the last four years. This is much lower than the ambition of India's education budget to be at 6 per cent of

GDP set out in the National Education Policy 2020. The proportion of total annual education spending has been around 10 per cent of total government expenditure across all sectors and dropped to below 10 per cent since 2020-21.

Comparison with some developed countries

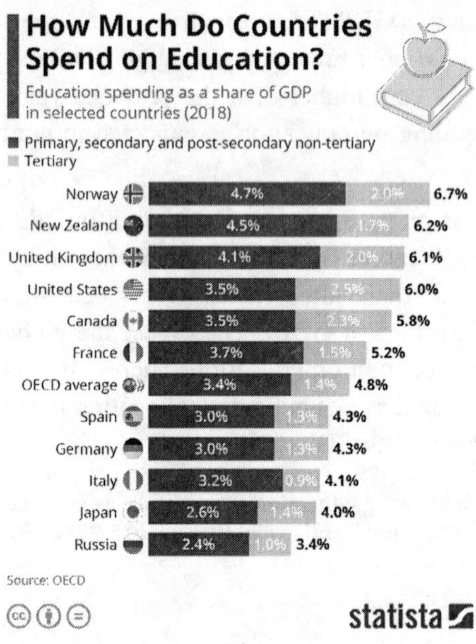

Source: OECD: Education at a glance.

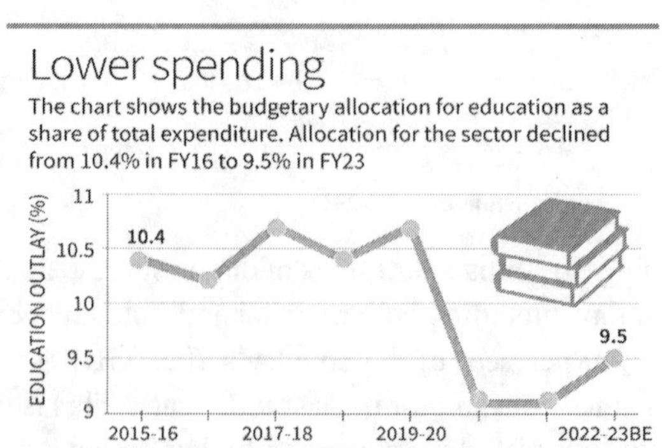

Source: Economic survey 2022-23.

Conclusion

The National Education Policy (NEP) of 2020 represents a significant milestone in India's journey towards revitalising its higher education system. By focusing on modernisation, innovation, and increased accessibility, the NEP aims to address longstanding structural challenges and adapt to evolving global educational trends. Through this study, we have identified key trends in budgetary allocation and expenditure in the higher education sector in India. The budget aims to improve learning and skill development in India. The impact of these budgetary changes will be felt across various dimensions of higher education, from institutional development and research capabilities to the overall quality of education. As institutions adapt to these new financial realities, their ability to innovate and strategically align with policy reforms will be crucial in navigating the challenges and seizing the opportunities.The future of higher education in India will depend on how effectively these adjustments are managed and how well the sector can leverage both the challenges and opportunities of the evolving financial landscape.

References

Agarwal, Pawan (2006), Higher Education in India: The need for a change. Working paper, no 180, Indian council for research on International Economic Relation (ICRIER), New Delhi.

Gupta, B.L. and Choubey, A.K., (2021), Higher Education institutions-some guidelines for obtaining and sustaining autonomy in the context of NEP 2020, International Journal of all research education and scientific methods (IJARESM) ISSN-2455-6211, Vol. 9, Issue 1, Jan.

Kurwar, N. and Chakraborty, S. (2013), Higher Education Scenario of the North-eastern India, PARIPEX-Indian Journal of Research, Vol. 2, Issue 3, pp. 78-80.

Mitra, A (2015), Public spending in Higher education in India: a benefit incidence analysis of higher education for future. 2(1), 71-79, the Kerela state higher education council, Sage Publication.

Sarkar and Koner S. (2018), Public expenditure on higher in India, International Journal of science and research (IJSR), ISSN: 2319-7064, Vol. 7, issue 11, Nov. 2018.

Chapter - 6

A Holistic and Multidisciplinary Education in Higher Education Institutions of Arunachal Pradesh with reference to NEP 2020

– Dr. Ligang Suniya, Miss Haj Morney, Miss Duyir Poyom

Abstract

In the 21st century, there is a significant need to comprehend developments in knowledge through the lens of disciplines as well as the dynamic interactions of discipline to find solutions to the problems of society. Hence, one of the key recommendations in the NEP 2020 is to establish large multidisciplinary higher education institutions in or near each district by 2030, to develop individuals' social, physical, intellectual, emotional, and moral qualities in an integrated way. A multidisciplinary higher education will feature many departments as well as creative multi-interdisciplinary courses to enable learners to broaden their thinking and learning capabilities and prepare them to meet new issues. In this paper, the researchers present their perspectives on multidisciplinary education in the context of higher education institution of Arunachal Pradesh.

Keywords: Multidisciplinary education, higher education institutions, holistic, and NEP 2020.

Introduction

Indian higher education has a long history, dating back to the original Vedic system of education. In the age of knowledge explosion, graduates must have mastery of their chosen disciplines and the current abilities necessary to compete in the world of tomorrow. The National Education Policy 2020 is the first education policy of the twenty-first century, to address our country's numerous expanding developmental requirements. This policy proposes revising and revamping all aspects of the education structure, including regulation and governance, to create a new system that is aligned with the aspirations of 21st-century education, including Sustainable Development Goal 4 (SDG4), while determining India's traditions and value systems. The National Educational Policy lays particular emphasis on the development of the creative potential of each individual. It is founded on the idea that education should foster not just cognitive abilities like critical thinking and problem-solving, but also social, ethical, and emotional qualities and dispositions. This type of learning may be accomplished through a comprehensive and diverse education. Holistic and interdisciplinary education would seek to develop all aspects of human potential in an integrated way, including intellectual, aesthetic, social, physical, emotional, and moral. Such an education will help in the development of well-rounded individuals who possess critical modern skills capacities in fields such as the arts, humanities, languages, sciences, social sciences, and professional, technical, and vocational fields, as well as a social engagement ethic, soft skills such as communication, discussion, and debate, and rigorous specialisation in a chosen field or fields.

NEP 2020: A holistic and Multidisciplinary Education in HEIs

Higher education, often regarded as the peak of academic study, marks a transformational period in the educational journeys of individuals while also driving the country toward progress. India has a lengthy heritage of holistic and interdisciplinary learning, as evidenced by institutions like Takshashila and Nalanda, as well as substantial Indian literature that combines themes from several areas. Ancient Indian literary works, such as Banabhatta's kadambari, defined a good education as knowledge of the 64 kalaas or arts, which included not only subjects such as singing and painting, but also scientific fields including chemistry and mathematics, vocational fields that include carpentry and clothing making, professional fields such as medicine and engineering, and soft skills like communication, discussion, and debate. The concept that all forms of creative human endeavour, including mathematics, physics, vocational disciplines, professional topics, and soft skills, should be deemed arts has distinct Indian roots. Our concept of understanding various arts or what is now often referred to as the liberal arts or a holistic and interdisciplinary education, is what is necessary in our century. A comprehensive and diverse education would benefit an individual's overall growth. It promotes the development of artistic, social, intellectual, physical, and moral abilities in an integrated manner. To achieve the goal of holistic and multidisciplinary education there needs to be setting up of large multidisciplinary universities and colleges. Higher education institutions will have more flexibility in establishing courses by being granted autonomy. More focus has to be placed on research, debate, communication, interpersonal skills, discussion, and possibilities for cross-disciplinary and interdisciplinary thinking. Therefore, the present research will concentrate on a holistic and multidisciplinary education in higher education institutions of Arunachal Pradesh.

Objectives of the Study

1. To explore the strategy for implementing holistic and multidisciplinary education in higher educational institutions (HEIs) as envisioned by NEP 2020.
2. To analyze the challenges related to implementing holistic and multidisciplinary education in higher educational institutions (HEIs) of Arunachal Pradesh.

Methodology

The present study is theoretical and solely based on secondary data obtained from research papers, articles, journals, websites, seminar reports, and commissions and committee reports.

The Strategy for Implementing Holistic and Multidisciplinary Education in HEIs under NEP 2020

The NEP 2020 aims to establish at least one significant multidisciplinary institution in or near each district by 2030. By 2040, all higher education institutions (HEIs) are expected to become multidisciplinary institutions with at least 3000 students. Thus, UGC develop a strategy for transforming all associated colleges into multidisciplinary higher education institutions as follow.

1. ***Transform stand alone institutions into multidisciplinary HEI:*** India has domain specific stand-alone college and universities. Even in multidisciplinary higher educational institutions the disciplinary boundaries are rigid that the opportunities to learn and explore different discipline are less explored. Therefore, NEP 2020 proposed to end this fragmentation of higher education is by transforming HEIs into multidisciplinary universities, colleges and knowledge hubs. The types of HEIs envisaged are: multidisciplinary research-intensive university, multidisciplinary teaching-intensive universities and degree awarding multi-disciplinary autonomous colleges. Flexibility in curriculum and novel and engaging course options will be on offer to students, in addition to rigorous specialisation in a subject/s. This will be encouraged by increase faculty and institutional autonomy in setting curricula. Pedagogy will have an increased emphasis on communication, discussion, debate, research, and opportunities for cross-disciplinary and interdisciplinary thinking. Departments in Languages, Literature, music, philosophy, indology, art, dance, theatre, education, mathematics, statistics, pure and applied sciences, sociology, economics, sports, translation and interpretation and other such subjects needed for a multidisciplinary, stimulating Indian education and environment will be established and strengthened at all Higher education Institutes (HEIs) Credits will be given in all Bachelor's Degree programmes for these subjects if they are done from such departments or through open and distance learning (OLD) mode when they are not offered in class at the higher education institute. The policy document has given that by 2035 all affiliated colleges should become degree-awarding multidisciplinary autonomous institutions.

2. ***Academic collaboration between HEIs:*** The NEP 2020 has been envisioned the academic collaboration of HEIs which will be under the purview of the affiliating universities in case they are willing to expand further by adding more programmes to strengthen the structure of multidisciplinary education. For the operational requirements, the physical proximity of the institutions should be such that they can share physical and human resources and ensure easier student and faculty mobility. The programmes should be offered with the idea of bringing flexibility and interdisicplinarity for the students. The institutions will have to enter into a written Memorandum of Understanding (MoU) with its partner institution(s) for collaboration.

    (i) ***Multiple Entry and Multiple Exit programme in UG courses and Dual Degree programmes:*** The Policy aims at 50% gross enrolment ratio by 2035. There will be multiple entry and exit options for those who wish to leave the course in the middle. Their credits will be transferred through Academic Bank of Credits (ABC). The undergraduate degree courses will be of either 3 or 4 year duration with multiple exit options.

    Collaboration between two institutions for the award of dual degree facilitates students enrolled in HEIs to take up the first degree at the host institution and the second degree at the partnering institution. A MoU may be signed between the partnering institutions to offer the dual degree with the approval of the university, the state government and/or the regulatory bodies, covering all aspects such as the number of seats, modalities of transition from one institution to another and awarding the degree. The feasibility in admission process, sharing hostel and other facilities, wherever possible, for the students between the partnering institutions.

3. ***The Colleges in the cluster:*** The existing colleges operating in the same campus or in close proximity can form a cluster.

This will ensure that colleges with poor enrolment and fewer resources can offer multidisciplinary programmes and can have access to better facilities for the benefit of all. The cluster colleges shall aim at making the courses more dynamic through collaboration with other universities, prestigious government institutions and reputed industrial houses and also avail of the courses offered in the online and ODL mode. In the case of private college forming a cluster, the trust, or society, or company which runs the college must be charitable and not-for-profit bodies. The board of directors provides overall direction and coordination of the cluster of colleges. The academic council works closely with the departments to develop new programmes and a research agenda and review the progress of research.

4. ***Autonomous Status of Colleges and Model HEIs:*** NEP 2020 envisioned the transformation of the affiliated colleges into autonomy leading to a degree-awarding institution and into a university. The member colleges in a cluster will continue to function as affiliated colleges under the university in the initial phase with the Board of Directors, Academic Council, Finance Committee and Curriculum Development Committee governing the academic, financial and administrative matters. During this phase, the member colleges may share their resources to offer multidisciplinary programmes and guide student research projects. After the initial years, the affiliating university may affiliate the cluster of colleges as a single unit. During this transformation phase, the cluster may pass through graded autonomy before developing into an autonomous degree granting cluster of college. With appropriate accreditations, autonomous degree-granting colleges can further evolve into Multidisciplinary research-intensive universities (RUs) and Multidisciplinary teaching-intensive universities (TUs).

Model public universities for holistic and multidisciplinary education, at par with IITs, IIMs, etc., called MERUs

(Multidisciplinary Education and Research Universities) will be set up and will aim to attain the highest global standards in quality education. They will also help set the highest standards for multidisciplinary education in the country.

5. ***Merger of HEIs under the same management and run by different managements:*** Institutions functioning under same managements may merge to put the academic and physical resources to optimal use and to optimal use and to offer multidisciplinary education. It will happen in accordance to the rules of the state government, affiliating university and / or the regulatory body.

   Further, a private institution desirous of merging with a single stream institution or multidisciplinary institution of another registered society or trust, may apply, with the approval of the affiliating university, to the society or trust of the institution to be merged with and become a part of it as per the procedure of the societies registration act or trust act.

6. ***Introduction of New Department:*** NEP 2020 emphasizes Adoption of diverse streams to fulfill the interest of the students providing them opportunities to choose from a variety of courses suiting their interest puts in place. The freedom to choose courses from a basket of courses paves way for a holistic development of the students thereby developing their mental, emotional, physical, and social skills. This helps the students to identify their uniqueness and align it with the world outside. For such the departments in Languages, Literature, music, philosophy, indology, art, dance, theatre, education, mathematics, statistics, pure and applied sciences, sociology, economics, sports, translation and interpretation and other such subjects recommended to introduce in higher educational institutions.

7. ***Opening of Education department in every HEIs:*** The NEP 2020 visualises establishment of one Education department

in colleges or universities or other HEIs to contribute to multidisciplinary and holistic education and to contribute to research and development in various aspects of education.

8. ***Flexible and Innovative Curriculum:*** Towards the attainment of such a holistic and multidisciplinary education, the flexible and innovative curricular structures will enable creative combinations of disciplines for study that would offer multiple entry and exit points and removing currently prevalent rigid boundaries and creating new possibilities for life-long learning. An Academic Bank of Credit (ABC) shall be established which would digitally store the academic credits earned from various recognised HEIs so that the degrees from an HEI can be awarded taking into account credits earned. Further, ODL (Open and Distance Learning) and online education provide a natural path to increase access to quality higher education. ODL programmes and online education framework, norms, standards and guidelines will be prepared by recommendatory for all HEIs will be developed.

9. ***Research in HEI Clusters:*** As the trend towards multi-disciplinary based research collaboration grows, it is imperative to train a new generation of teacher researches in the multidisciplinary research areas. For this a Multidisciplinary Research Committee comprising members from collaborating institutions may be formed. It also recommends by NEP 2020 to collaborate between HEI clusters in students projects and with industries and/ or government and non-government organisations.

10. ***Role of Parent University:*** To identify potentials of colleges and to encourage them by providing timely approval to their proposals and help to nominate representatives in various committees for the proper functioning of cluster colleges and enable collaboration between institutions.

11. ***Establishing regulatory bodies:*** The role and responsibilities of regulatory bodies are very crucial in order to monitor the quality of higher education institutions. As mentioned in the policy document, the regulatory systems are in need of a complete overhaul in order to re-energies the higher education sector and enable it to believe. Thus, the policy document, has suggested four regulatory bodies to be set up as four independent verticals working within one umbrella institution called Higher Education Commission of India (HECI) namely: National Higher Education Regulatory Council (NHERC), National Accreditation Council (NAC), Higher Education Grants Council (HEGC) and General Education Council (GEC). These four regulatory bodies will ensure the distinct functions of regulation, accreditation, funding and academic standard setting. The policy also recommended for establishing National Research Foundation (NRF) to facilitate a conducive research environment in universities and colleges by providing research grants and infrastructure through different programmes. The present Nationational Assessment and Accredition Council (NAAC) can be renamed as National Accreditation Council (NAC), it will act like Meta Accreditation body in charge of accreditation of institutions and NTA to offer common entrance exam (CUET).

Challenges in Implementing Holistic and Multidisciplinary Education in Higher Educational Institutions, Arunachal Pradesh

Some of the challenges that may be encountered when adopting NEP 2020's holistic and multidisciplinary education in the state's HEIs are outlined below.

1. **Execution of the policy:** According to the Director of Higher and Technical Education (2020), the Government of Arunachal Pradesh reports that the state has only 62 higher and technical institutions, including 18 government degree

colleges and 12 universities (comprising central, state, deemed, and private universities). The policy statement indicates that providing multidisciplinary education in the state will be challenging due to the limited number of institutions and their distance from one another.

2. **Lack of adequate infrastructural facilities.** Lack of academic facilities and infrastructures, including technology-enabled and assisted learning ecosystems, which include video-based classes, infrastructure for blended and online learning modes, other academic infrastructure such as library and laboratories infrastructure for differently-abled students, facilities and infrastructure for faculty, and infrastructure for promoting sports and wellness, and the arts, will prevent institutions leading to multidisciplinary institutions. Many state-run higher education institutions are operating without adequate staffing, facilities, dormitories, libraries, transportation, labs, and staff housing. In the lack of suitable facilities, quality progress, and multidisciplinary education are impossible. It observes that majority of higher education institutions in Arunachal Pradesh have basic facilities and infrastructure. Implementing the holistic and multidisciplinary education will be highly challenging.

3. **Lack of scientific and technological institutions for partnering humanities stream.** Arunachal Pradesh has a countable number of technical and professional institutes. Moreover, many students are admitted to general education institutions, mostly for humanities courses. In this circumstance, the student will unable to take any scientific or technology.

4. **The Cluster colleges.** The concept of cluster colleges in hilly states, such as Arunachal Pradesh, will face unique challenges due to their geographic and infrastructural conditions. These challenges include geographic accessibility issues, with many colleges located in remote or difficult-to-reach areas that complicate transportation and access for

students and faculty. Weather conditions, such as heavy rainfall and landslides during the monsoon season, further disrupt travel and accessibility. Infrastructure limitations are also prevalent, with cluster colleges often needing more facilities, including insufficient classroom space, laboratories, and libraries. Poor connectivity limits internet access and communication, hindering the implementation of modern educational technologies and distance learning.

5. **Shortage of teachers:** In the state, most higher education institutions have had vacant faculty positions in various departments that have not been filled for years. To address this issue, part-time contractual, guest lecturer, and other positions are appointed with minimal remuneration. This lays an adverse effect on multidisciplinary education in HEIs.

6. **Less allocation of finance:** It is a key issue of development of higher educational institutions. The Indian government spends 4.43% of GDP on education (Economic Survey 2017-2018). As such, many higher education institutions are struggling to exist with inadequate infrastructure. Although NEP 2020 proposed allocating 6% of GDP to education, just 3% has been allocated. The budget was reduced by 6% in 2021-22. Adequate financial resources should be provided to the education sector. Furthermore, higher education institutions should use strategic human resource management strategies.

7. **Practicability experiential learning:** NEP 2020 openly challenges the rigid curriculum and rote learning system which is continuing from a decade. Thus, it will be difficult for the stakeholders of education to shift from memorisation to critical thinking and experiential learning in a holistic and multidisciplinary education. Moreover, the biggest challenges for the stakeholders are the articulation and delivery of the amended curriculum and pedagogy at ground level.

8. **Schedule for Programmes or Courses:** It will be tough to plan curricular timetables with other departments or partner universities so that students can take various courses in the programme. However, only successful collaboration, cooperation, and partnership across all higher education institutions are required to overcome the barriers and make the policy a huge success. Another important consideration is the amount of time and effort necessary for a multidisciplinary curriculum. Unlike traditional education, which concentrates on a particular subject, this approach aims to develop the whole person. Therefore, developing a curriculum that meets the unique requirements of children can be time-consuming and challenging.
9. **Lack of awareness** among students, teachers, parents, and stakeholders about the benefits of multidisciplinary education challenges the implementation of the policy.
10. **Political divisiveness** poses a problem in implementing the large policy. The failure of the centre to bridge trust with the states is a major hurdle in the path of success.

Suggestions for Implementation of a Multidisciplinary Approach in HEIs

Arunachal Pradesh being a region of multisided diversities, its development is impeded by certain inherent difficulties such as inadequate infrastructure, adverse climatic conditions and mountainous landscape. It is needless to mention that quality higher education is pre-requisite for creation and development of skilled human resources. These are some suggestions for improving the quality of higher education institutions so that they can grow into multidisciplinary institutions, as stated below:

- With guidance from experts, the state stakeholders should develop a comprehensive plan for holistic and multidisciplinary education in higher education institutions, taking into consideration the existing facilities, infrastructure, staff, and unique geographical and climatic circumstances.

- Relevant curriculum, effective pedagogical strategies, and assessment methodologies for multidisciplinary education in higher education institutions should be developed with the help of experts from various fields.
- To bridge the gap between physical and e-learning, a bottom-up strategy should include technology-enhanced training to all educational stakeholders.
- Financial assistance should be increased to acquire adequate educational infrastructure in higher education institutions in Arunachal Pradesh, such as books, journals, study materials, audio-visual facilities, e-resources, virtual classrooms, and high-bandwidth internet connectivity, to effectively deliver courses through ODL (Open and Distance Learning), online education, etc.
- To reduce personnel shortages and enhance overall institutional functioning, the stakeholder should ensure sufficient appointment of teaching and non-teaching staff in higher education institutions.
- Internet facilities should be improved by directing service providers to construct towers near higher education institutions that are poorly served
- To effectively implement holistic multidisciplinary education at higher education institutions, stakeholders, administrators, teachers, students, and parents should be made aware of NEP 2020 through awareness activities.

Discussion and Conclusion

The introduction of multidisciplinary education under NEP 2020 is an extremely comprehensive document that has created a lot of space to restructure and change the Indian education system to compete with some of the advanced countries. This approach to learning looks at how different disciplines can interact and overlap with each other to create a comprehensive understanding of a subject. With a holistic and multidisciplinary education every child is endowed with multiple intelligence and can grasp multiple subjects according to the interest and the available opportunity that promotes understanding of a wide variety of subjects that support more of their intelligences and help them become successful. As the policy document stated of setting up at least one large multidisciplinary institution in or near every district by the year 2030. Every higher education institution must equip itself with highly qualified individuals capable of offering such an approach, as well as guarantee that the appropriate resources are available. However, it appears that the concept that this type of education can be accomplished with the present curriculum and resources is a mere myth. Academicians and policymakers have a huge task in restructuring the present curriculum to transform ideas into actions that result in substantial improvements and contribute to the knowledge economy of the country.

References

Sharma, S.C. & Swamy, S.S., "Roadmap for holistic implementation of the National Education Policy-2020", *Association of Indian Universities*, New Delhi, India, 2021.

Patra, R.R. & Nandi, R.K., "Higher education as per NEP-2020: Key highlights, implementation status, challenges, and suggestions", *Journal of Emerging Technologies and Innovative Research (JETIR),* February 2023, Vol(10), Issue (2).

Bashir, L. & Wani, G., "Multidisciplinary and holistic education: Achieving academic excellence and bolstering all-round development in the 21st century with NEP-2020", *The International Journal of Indian Psychology*, March, 2024, Vol (12), Issue (1), https//www.ijip.in

Roy, M., "A critical study on the holistic and multidisciplinary approach of National Educational Policy 2020 (NEP 2020) in India", *International Journal for Multidisciplinary Research (IJFMR),* December, 2022, Vol(4), Issue(6), www.Ijfmr.com

Shukla, B., Joshi, M., Sujatha, R., Beena, T., & Kumar, H., "Demystifying approaches of holistic and multidisciplinary education for diverse career opportunities: NEP 2020", *Indian Journal of Science and Technology,* April, 2022, https://www.indjst.org/

Gurchal, M.G., &Yamdagini, P., "Multidisciplinary and holistic approach in higher education with reference to NEP:2020", *International Journal of Advanced Research in Science, Communication and Technology (IJARSCT)*, April 2022, Vol (2), Issue(5).

Prakash, G.S.U., & Ibrahim S.M.K., "National Education Policy-2020: Milestone towards strengthening holistic and multidisciplinary education in India", *International journal of Science and Research (IJSR),* September 2021, Vol(10), Issue (9), www.ijsr.net

Sharma, A.K., Solanki, S.P.H. & Chomal, S., "Holistic and multidisciplinary education approaches in higher education NEP 2020", *International Journal for Research in Applied Science & Engineering Technology (IJRASET),* February 2024, Vol (12), Issue II, www.ijraset.com

Guidelines for multiple entry and exit in academic programmes offered in higher education institutions. UGC, New Delhi, July 2021.

Guidelines for transforming higher education institution into multidisciplinary institutions, UGC, New Delhi, September, 2022.

NEP 2020. Ministry of Human Resource Development, Government of India, 2020.

Chapter - 7

Issues and Challenges of Teacher Education in India with Special Reference to National Education Policy 2020

– Geyin Miyu & Kigo Raksap

Abstract

Recently, India is encountering quick and sudden changes in teacher education. The one -year B.Ed. Programme was converted into a two-year Programme in 2015, and it was implemented abruptly and without much planning in the same year. While the stakeholders of teacher education are still busy in reflecting and debating the pros and cons of 2-year B.Ed. programme, NEP 2020 has declared that from 2030 the Integrated Teacher Education Programme (ITEP) i.e. the 4-Year Integrated B.Ed. Programme will be the lone teacher education programme in the country for preparing secondary education teachers. It appears that teacher education is in the midst of a significant transformation. Teacher educators, pupil-teachers, and all other stakeholders are unsure what will happen and, if implemented, how it will be carried out in B.Ed. colleges and universities' departments of teacher education. The vision and mission of teacher education, which directs and decides the fate of school education, must be crystal clear. The main focus of this paper is to discuss the issue and current challenges and to forecasts some possible solutions to the issues and challenges confronting teacher education in the country.

Keywords: Issues and challenges, Teacher Education, National Education Policy 2020, B.Ed Programme.

Introduction

Teacher Education has always been an important component of education since time immemorial. This is because all societies in the world have always needed teachers to propagate/transmit their cultures from one generation to another. Teachers need to be seen as creators of knowledge and thinking professionals. A teacher needs to be an information provider, role model, facilitator, assessor, planner, resource and developer.

Educated teachers, with wide knowledge, command the respect of fellow teachers and the people in their communities. They need to be empowered to recognise and value what children learn from their home, social and cultural environment and to create opportunities for children to discover, learn and develop. Teacher is a facilitator, is a friend, and is a philosopher.

The purpose of teacher education programme should be to develop in each student his general education and personal culture, his ability to teach and educate others, an awareness of the principles which underlines good human relations and a sense of the responsibility to contribute both by teaching and leading as an example to social, cultural and economic progress. The nation building task will be performed under the leadership of a brilliant set of teacher educators and master educators who will prepare the teachers and who in turn will develop the creative abilities of the teeming millions of the country.

In 2020, the Indian Ministry of Education introduced the National Education Policy (NEP) 2020, replacing the 34-year-old National Policy on Education, 1986. Along with the many reforms in the policy to strengthen higher education in the country, the NEP mandated accreditation of all state-run schools from grade 1 to 12.

Accreditation is a process carried out to improve the standards of education, outcomes, and governance of schools. It looks at measures such as the quality of teaching, attendance, number of teachers across subjects and grades, safety, financial probity, curriculum, basic sustainable infrastructure, resources, community participation, governance process, and accountability. A fair, transparent, and rigorous accreditation and evaluation process can enable education systems to change the academics, management, and leadership of institutions for the better.

National Education Policy-2020 has reaffirmed the role of teacher as the fulcrum of desired transformations. Starting with the vision of developing an equitable and just society to empowering the nation to face new set of challenges posed by the 'new world order' and global ecosystem, the teacher remains the catalyst of change. The lofty ideals envisaged in the policy including universal access to holistic quality education, life-long learning opportunities for all, constructive revamping of aspirational goals of 21st century education and regaining the status of Visva-Guru in true sense of the word, shall see the light of the day with active participation of teaching community not only as the disseminator of knowledge but also as the most vital stakeholder to develop highlevel foundational, creative, cognitive, social, ethical and emotional capacities among individual learners.

The National Education Policy-2020 envisions the teacher to imbibe all the spiritual, professional and ethical attributes of an ideal mentor and guide for the students, which makes it imperative for the students, parents, governments and other stakeholders to rethink their attitude towards the lesser acknowledged warrior in the mission of constructive social change. It also motivates us to derive inspiration from the great Indian visionary teachers such as Swami Dayanand Saraswati, Rabindra Nath Tagore, Swami Vivekananda, Savitribai Phule, Premchand, Dr Sarvepalli Radhakrishnan, Dr APJ Abdul Kalam and many others who dedicated their entire life in the service of the nation. Considering teaching as the noblest profession, Kalam rightly observed that "If the people remember me as a good teacher that will be the biggest honour for me".

The National Education Policy (NEP) 2020 is a comprehensive reform that aims to transform the education system in India, including higher education. It focuses on multidisciplinary education, flexibility in curriculum, and promoting research. The National Policy on Education (NPE) 1986 was a previous education policy that emphasized universalisation of elementary education and reducing disparities. Both policies have contributed to shaping India's education landscape, with NEP 2020 building upon the foundation laid by NPE 1986.

According to the Justice J. S. Verma' Commission (2012) constituted by the Supreme Court, a majority of stand-alone TEIs - over 10,000 in number are not even attempting serious teacher education but are essentially selling degrees for a price. Regulatory efforts so far have neither been able to curb the malpractices in the system, nor enforce basic standards for quality, and in fact have had the negative effect of curbing the growth of excellence and innovation in the sector. The sector and its regulatory system are, therefore, in urgent need of revitalisation through radical action, in order to raise standards and restore integrity, credibility, efficacy, and high quality to the teacher education system.

Main aim of NEP 2020

NEP, 2020 aim to increase the Gross Enrolment Ratio (GER) to 100% in preschool to secondary level by 2030 whereas GER in Higher Education including vocational education from 26.3% (2018) to 50% by 2035. Today if the world is inclined to seek a long term means to build and promote peace on this planet earth, we have to opt for education and ultimately we should go for teachers as they will contribute by performing their role in building and promoting culture of peace among children / students and in their institutional environment that will further extend peace to the community, society, nation and lastly to the world. This is high time when Teacher Education programmes should combine knowledge, experiences and dreams pertaining to the building of peace and harmony on one hand, and joint effort of other people and agencies of education on the other, in such a way so as to change the culture of war to culture of peace and non violence in the world we live in. The present paper discusses the role of teacher education in promoting Peace and harmony among the people for a better and happy living.

Role of teachers recommended by NEP 2020

1. Passionate and Motivated

2. Creating Classroom
3. Well Qualified and Trained Content
4. Mentoring and Facilitator
5. Pedagogy and Practice
6. Parameters of Quality Concerns the Topic
7. Knowledge about the subject.
8. Teaching Learning environment.
9. Curriculum and Teaching Learning material
10. Teachers participation with demands and changing society
11. Management and curriculum support
12. Develop quality culture in the institution.
13. Teachers accountability and responsibility
14. Positive reinforcement

Purpose of the NEP for Teacher Education

The objective of the policy is to achieve a community of competent teachers dedicated to providing education of high quality, with high levels of performance as well as ethical and professional standards of conduct.

NEP 2020 for Teachers Recruitment

The New Education Policy aims to help recruit the very best and brightest to enter the teaching profession at all levels, by ensuring teachers their livelihood, respect, dignity, and autonomy, while also installing in the system basic methods of quality control and accountability. The National Education Policy states that by 2030 the minimum educational qualification for teachers would be a four-year duration integrated BEd degree. If this happens, only candidates with a four-year BEd degree and CTET or TET certificate will be eligible to apply for teacher recruitment in government schools.

Teachers truly shape the future of our children - and, therefore, the future of our nation. (NEP 2020)

Challenges and issues of Teacher Education in NEP 2020 are:

Accepting Change in Teaching – Learning Styles:

The new NEP has suggested many new methods of dealing with children of different age groups right from the pre-primary stage to higher education. Making such arrangements at each school and college to adopt such a holistic development for teachers might become an obstacle as they were used to old methods of delivering lectures. So, this shift from old methods to modern scenarios may prove a problem for both students and teachers. The students in our country cannot afford such grasping knowledge and the lack of resources would burden them and their parents.

Trained teacher educators:

These multidisciplinary institutions will need to hire specific subject professors and teacher educators depending upon the requirement. Teacher educators need to teach specific age groups (Std.-12 passed teenagers). Reduction in entry-level qualification (graduate level to std 12th) needs to be considered and training should be given accordingly to teacher educators.

Traditional and Theoretical Curriculum:

The new education policy has made various recommendations to reform teacher education but no new curriculum has been developed in that. The current curriculum of teacher education is traditional and the theoretical curriculum lacks practical prospects.

Duration of Course:

The one year of teacher education in the new education policy is being especially criticized. During this one year, the theoretical and practical aspects of the teacher education curriculum will fall and the students will face problems regarding the internship. The national curriculum framework (1998) also recommends the two-year duration of teacher education programmes but could not implement them. So, there is a need to extend the period of the present teacher education programme.

Lack of control over teacher education institutions:

NCTE is a supervisory body that panels the operative of teacher education institutions and holds control over the quality of education there. It circles and continues the standards of education in these institutions. But in the past few years teacher education institutions have so extremely increased in number that it becomes difficult to monitor all the institutions. Some of these institutions are compromising on quality and standards for the sake of monetary benefits only.

Lack of Innovation and Creativity:

Creativity plays an important role while performing any task. But this factor is ignored while delivering knowledge in teacher education programmes today.

Lack of development of Life Skills:

Life skills are certain skills that are essential for personal development and growth. These skills enable man to deal with life's difficulties. The main issue is that teacher education is memory based i.e. there is no active involvement of students, so there is a lack in the development of life skills among the students, which are essential for the round development of students.

Quality Issues:

Teacher education has not come up to the requisite standards. Teachers are not able to think critically and solve problems related to teaching methods, content, organisations, etc. More knowledge of theoretical principles is emphasized and teachers are not able to apply these principles in actual classroom situations.

Problem of teaching practice: This is one of the main problems of teacher education. Teaching practice is neither adequate nor properly conducted. The student teacher does not take the task of teaching practice seriously. Also, on the other side, the school and school management pose problems as they do not cooperate and do not get ready to allow teaching practice sessions. They do not allow proper implementation of the teaching practice.

Lack of proper facilities:

A large number of education colleges have unhealthy financial conditions. They lack basic facilities such as experimental schools, laboratories, libraries, hostels, and proper and safe buildings. Some of them even are running in rented buildings.

Suggestions for Improving the Condition of Teacher Education:

- The government has set itself an ambitious goal of improving the quality of teacher education. They want to ensure that all teachers are well-trained and knowledgeable about their subjects. This means that teachers need to have a deep understanding of the content they teach, as well as how students learn best.
- The curriculum needs to be revised and updated. This can be a lengthy process, especially considering that it has not been updated since the 1990s. Teachers need to be well-trained in the subjects they teach.
- They need to be able to understand how students learn best and what strategies can be used to ensure that learning happens.
- The government wants to move away from a "teacher training" model to one that focuses on teacher "education". This will require a lot of changes in the way teachers are trained, including the curriculum and how it is designed.
- New and innovative techniques can be used for the transaction of the curriculum.
- The teacher education programme should be modified so that teachers are equipped for the different roles and functions imposed by new technologies.
- Teachers should train about stress management mechanisms so that they could help students in managing their stress and sustaining themselves in this time of social isolation,

parental pressure, etc. Teachers should be able to think critically make the right decisions and maintain harmonious relation with others.

- Techniques used in teaching should develop a habit of self-learning and reduce dependence on teachers. It will help them to reflect on their own and do something new.
- There is a need for a specific time frame for the improvement of private teacher education institutes and those teacher educational institutions which are weak in terms of infrastructure and teaching equipment.

Conclusion

Education gives a new shape to the individual and the nation as well. It is a wellknown saying that a teacher is a nation-builder. No doubt a lot of stress is given to teacher-education courses in India. Unfortunately, still, there are several loopholes in the system. In light of NEP 2020, the time has come for Indian teachers to grab the opportunity and become makers of their intentions. They need to dream and work hard to achieve them. The National Education Policy will play an important role in taking the education system to a new level and is extremely important in maintaining the quality of the education system. It will help to present the education system of India in an outstanding context. However, it is important to emphasize how quickly the implementation of the new education policy is possible and how the new education policy can be implemented by solving the various problems of the previous education before implementing it.

References

Bhatt, T. (2022), New Education Policy 2020 Challenges and Opportunities for Teacher Education, Neuro Quantology, 20(20), 3414-3419 doi:10.14704/nq.2022.20.13. NQ88421.

Jadhav, N. (2022), Issues and Challenges of National Education Policy (NEP) 2020 implementation in Teacher Education, International Journal of Enhanced Research in Educational Development (IJERED), 10(3), 188-191. Retrieved fromhttps://www.researchgate.net/publication/362538441.

Kumari, S. (2020), NEP 2020 Challenges to Teachers Education, International Journal of Applied Research, 6(10), 420-424. Retrieved from https://www.allresearchjournal.com/archives/?year=2020&vol=6&issue=10&part=G&ArticleId=7 339.

Sharma, S. & Kumar, T. (2020), Problems and Opportunities in Teacher Education in the Context of National Education Policy 2020, International Journal for Research Trends and Innovation, 7(7), Retrieved from https://ijrti.org/papers/IJRTI2207236.pdf.

Chapter - 8

Challenges of Teacher Education in NEP -2020

– ***Mrs. Yuton Lhamu***

Abstract

Since first rolling out the National policy of Education 1986, the Prime minister of India Shri Narendra Modi made his first speech in the parliament on 11th June 2014. Expressing his vision of transforming the education system came true through the New Education Policy on 29th July 2020. The pillars of this policy are Access, Equity, Quality, Affordability and Accountability. The policy aims to transform India's education System by 2030. The new Education Policy (NEP) 2020 brought drastic changes in existing educational system from Priprimary to higher education. Consequently, there is a strong move to revise the structure of teacher education. Teachers' cognition, dedication, teaching techniques, professional approach and his intrinsic motivation are responsible factors needed for qualitative teaching-learning process. Production of competent and effective teachers is a big challenge in the modern world. Teacher education need to be formulated and implemented. So, the policy recommends major changes in the teacher education scenario in chapter-15 of NEP under part-II which is divided into eleven sub-points. The main objectives of NEP is to "ensure that teachers are given the highest quality training in content, pedagogy and practice, by moving the teachers education system into multi-disciplinary colleges and universities, and establishment the four year integrated B.Ed. offered by such multidisciplinary HEIs will, by 2030 become the minimal degree qualification for school teacher" (NEP2020 page 42:15.5). The policy seeks to ensure that all students at all stages of schooling are protected. With the advancement of growing technology and increasing knowledge, today's teacher job has become more challenging in pedagogical and psychological theories, philosophical and sociological perspective. So, necessary improvement in teacher education is a challenge for a nation to provide competent and qualified teacher. However, the purpose of the paper is an attempt to highlight some of the challenges of teacher education in the light of NEP-2020.

Keywords:- Education policy, NEP 2020, Teacher Education Challenges.

Introduction

Education is the key for any development of society which depends on the quality of teachers. It also plays a major role in bringing social change, economic and political development of any society. Education helps people to learn right action at right time. Such an education requires efficient teachers. It is a well-known saying that teachers build nation. Teachers is the central figures in the formal teaching - learning process. Students futures are dependent on their teachers. The teacher is regarded as the most important element in the educational system. It is the teacher, who is responsible for putting into practice the entire educational programme at any stage. It is vital to make investment in upgrading the skills, technique and quality of the teacher in an appropriate manner, so that the individual, community as well as entire nation can move forward into progression. Teacher performance is the most crucial input in the field of education. The importance of teacher in a society can never be underestimated therefore, for developing the quality of teacher, teacher education is vital in creating a pool of school teacher that will shape the next generation. The quality of teacher education programme is need to be upgraded. Teacher preparation is an activity that requires multidisciplinary outlook and knowledge, formation of dispositions and value, and development of practice under best mentor. Teachers must be grounded in Indian values, languages, knowledge, ethics and tradition including tribal traditions while also being well versed in the latest advance in pedagogy and education. To imbibe all the values, the society need highly qualified, well trained motivated and determined teachers to ensure meaningful access to education. Creation of such competent and an effective teacher is a big challenge in the modern world. With the increasing knowledge, today's teachers job has been more challenging in pedagogical, psychological philosophical and sociological perspective teacher are not able to think critically and solve the issue related to teaching methods, content, organisation etc. Teacher Education programme needs a extensive mending and restructuring curriculum of teacher-education programme needs to revised according to changing needs of society. Unfortunately, there are several loopholes in the system. Both centre and state government should join the hands to bring the quality and improvement in the teacher education, then the bright future of teacher education is possible.

Objective:- To discuss the Challenges of Teacher Education in NEP 2020.

REVIEW OF RELATED LITERATURE

Kumari (2020) studied on NEP-2020 Challenges to Teacher Education, the study revealed that there are many loopholes in education system and also suggest that the centre and state government should work together for bringing quality and improvement in teacher education.

Basanti Mohanti (2023) carried out a study with the objective of discussing the challenges of teacher education towards NEP 2020. In this study showed that the implementation of the New Education Policy is possible if it will enhance the quality of teacher education and present the teacher education system in world class environment with opening challenging and suggestion for enforcing the recommendation of teacher education.

Jadhav Netaji (2022) conducted a research on Issues and challenges of NEP 2020 implementation in Teacher education. The findings revealed that new education policy is going to be helpful for our nation India and surely take us on a new path of hope.

Borah Sobitri (2024) studied with the objectives to find out the challenges in teacher education. The study showed that teacher education can build favourable attitude in teacher -student towards the teaching profession and acquaints a future with all the latest innovation and developments.

Puranjoy Sonowal (2024) conducted a study to examine teacher education in NEP 2020: its challenges and opportunities. The study identifies some of the challenges facing by teacher education in the light of teacher education.

METHODOLOGY:- The method of this paper is descriptive in nature and required information are collected from different secondary sources like books, journals, articles, written documents and the internet.

CHALLENGES OF TEACHER EDUCATION IN NEP- 2020

In general teacher education needs urgent and complete reform. There is a need for more convergence in terms of level, duration and organisation between professional preparation and continuous professional development of teachers at all stage of schooling. One of the main issues that teachers faced and a good teachers dares to tackle all of these challenges boldly. Here we take a look at some of the most common challenges that teachers encounter in today's educational institutions.

- *A lot of paper work*

  Besides, to preparing for quality teaching content, it is common for school management to hand them with many additional roles including psycho-education, school worker, counsellor and many more. Overburden paper works needs lots of time which is away from regular timetable. So this can have a significant impact on the quality of work they produce

- *Teacher Training*

  The policy emphasizes the need the teacher training and development, but there are several challenges in implementing this. The existing teacher education system needs to be redesigned to meet the changing needs of the education system.

- *Lack of Innovation and creativity*

  Creativity plays an important role while performing any task. But this factor is ignored while delivering knowledge in teacher-education programmes today.

- *Balancing Diverse learning needs*

  In a classroom, every individual student will be different and they will have diverse learning needs. It will be a serious challenge to satisfying all of them in the same way while approaching a particular.

- *Stagnant Technical Device*

  This is an emerging technical gap in the system of education. Though virtual classrooms have become a window of hope to the educational system, it has also been difficult teachers when it comes to using it in their real lives.

- *Changing Educational Trends*

  The main classroom challenges faced by teacher is that educational trends have been changing every year. Schools will be eager to adopt new technologies and tools to update new trends. Teacher will have to figure out how effectively they can utilise the new tools. This can result in inconsistency in their teaching styles and more often leading to frustration and low job satisfaction. Familiarisation to new tools and technique needs time and dedication to which teacher educator has to adjust their schedule which is time consuming.

- *Applying a prescribed curriculum to all types of students.*

  It is a known fact that each student is different. But problems arise when a specific curriculum is prescribed for all students. The pace of understanding a concept differs from child to child. Situation turns crucial when teachers are expected to apply a fixed curriculum to students with varying needs. Teacher also don't get enough time to tailor content appealingly as per the needs of students.

- *Textbooks exposure to learning*

  Teachers are informed to follow the textbooks and teach by keeping a vision on final examination that the student have to go through. This led to a situation where teachers teach and student learn only what is prescribed in textbook.

- *The multi entry and exit concept*

  The concept is very interesting but it can create an issue for maintaining a record of the student who will join the education at any time and leave at any level will create a problem for keeping the track record of those as it is seen when stream system too dissolved, as it was to recognize from looking at the score card whether which student will belong to which stream. This problem may trouble the higher educational institutes to implement such policy

- *Lack of Self-time*

  The whole day long teachers do multitask for an effective teaching -learning process. And often teacher are forced to neglect their own bodies. They won't go for refreshment in between. There is even hectic schedule, where they even skip lunch. They use their own spare time in familiarising themself to new technology and tool thereby not taking time to relax their mind.

- *Changing in Teaching-Learning styles*

  The NEP has suggested many new methods of dealing with children of different age groups right from the Pre-primary to higher education. Making such arrangement at each school and college to adopt such a holistic development for teacher might become an obstacle as they were used to old methods of delivering lectures. So, the sudden shift from old method to modern may prove a problem for both student and teachers. The student of country like India cannot afford such grasping knowledge and the lack of resources would burden them and their parents.

- *Lack of proper infrastructure*

  A large number of colleges have unhealthy financial condition. They lack basic facilities such as experimental, school, laboratories, libraries, hostel and proper and safe building. Even some of teacher training institute are running in rented buildings. This not just affect the teaching process but also the quality of teaching.

- *Teachers being made responsible for more than they should*

  Most of the time teachers don't feel that the responsibility is equally shared between them, parents and students. Unfortunately, they will have bear a lot of responsibilities on their shoulders.

- *Differentiating and personalising Teaching*

  What works for one student does not work for the other. Teachers are clear about this and are looking for newer ways to analyse and evaluate different skill level. Media-enhanced exams, newer question types etc are some of the changes that teachers are looking for. Diversifying teaching methods. But keeping it simple is the right solution, but it is hard to execute.

- *Lack of science and technology*

  With the advancement of science and technology the world has become interdependent and is gradually turning into a global village. But educational programme for teachers or teacher-education have not made full use of latest technologies for developing teaching skills among students. Theoretical and traditional methods still prevalent in the teacher education institute.

- *Orientation to Teacher towards multidisciplinary education*

  The existing education system excludes formal training and orientation towards pedagogy for college and university educators. The policy seeks to establish multi-disciplinary institution ones. The road to attain this goal has been paved with intentions. For this purpose, there is need for proper training teacher-educator. Teacher-educators are competent to deal with problem of classroom and behaviour problem of student teachers and are not efficient enough to develop desired level of skills among the student teachers. They have lack of subject-matter mastery. NEP 2020 implementing such bold objectives will require training teachers, educator and official staff appropriately.

- *Lack of trained and skillfull teacher*

  One of the major setbacks of Indian education system is the lack of trained and skillful teachers who may engaged the student in various dimensions and develop innovative and scientific temper in them. Since they themselves lack of training, quality, innovation etc giving them the task to inculcate the student with this qualities is a mirage.

- Changing the mindset of stakeholders

  Our present education system is the practice of the British and Industrial age. The change in mindset will involve two or more generation of parents, teachers, grandparents and educators. A STEM education focused generation has to give way to the NEP. The corporate world also will need to align this and change its recruitment and grooming policies. There will be several challenges in changing this mindset. However, it can be done with lot of soft power play by the government.

- *Control over Teacher Education Institutions*

  The teacher education regulatory bodies need be empowered to take stringent action against substandard and dysfunctional teacher education institution (TEIs) that do not meet basic educational criteria. NCTE is regulatory body which controls the functioning of teacher education institutions and holds control over the quality education there. It sets and maintains the standards of education in these institutions. But in past few years teacher education institution are so drastically i (2022), Issues and challenges of educational policy (NEP) 2020 tation in Teacher Education, *International Journal of Enhanced in Educational Development,* Vol. 10 (3).

ek, Mr. Ravindranath Sanam, 2023, [NEP2020 – A new paradigm eacher Education. *International journal of Education, Modern ent, Applied Science & Social Science* (IJEMMASSS) Vol. 05

u, NEP 2020, Issues and challenges Ahead in Teacher education, *ernational journal Indian Psychology,* Vol. (11)

awal (2024), *Teacher Education in Northeast India* ISBN-978-81- pp. 93-94.

i (2020), [NEP2020-challenges to Teacher Education *International Applied Research,* Vol. 6 (10) 420-424.

020), National Education Policy NEP-2020, Opportunities and s on Teacher education. *International Journal of Management*), 1881-1886.

av (2022), Challenges in Teacher Education in the context of Education Policy, Higher Education and Teacher skills for NEP *ternational journal of Emerging Technologies and innovative* Vol. 9(10) a764.

increase in number that becomes difficult to monitor all the institutions. Some of these institutions are compromising quality for the sake of money only.

- *Inspiring students to be more Self- Directed*

  Teachers face a hard time in getting students to be more self-directed. They are looking for ways to reduce the pressure of students by evoking interest and curiosity in young minds.

- *Lack of Time for planning*

  Contrary in the past when teachers can't just finish off their syllabus and assessed them typically but today the situation is more challenging. They will have to handle multiple roles in the classroom. Teachers are finding it really challenging to handle multiple roles as they lack enough them for planning.

- *Teachers working too many roles at the same time*

  More than a teacher. Either he /she should take up the role of a social worker, counsellor, psycho-educator, or more at times. They are expected to shoulder different roles throughout the day.

- *Availability of Employment Opportunities*

  The NEP 2020 implementation will also be a slight create a challenge in employment industry as all new young people who are graduated will rush into the market for seeking jobs with high expected packages. So, the industry too should be able to create jobs in variety to fulfil their dreams, otherwise educated people's unemployment ratio might increase which increase which will also harm nation's progress.

SUGGESTIONS

Suggestive measures for improving the condition of teacher education –

- The curriculum needs to be revised and updated. Teacher needs to be well trained in the subject they teach.

- Teacher should be able to think critically make right decision and maintain harmonious relation with others.
- The Government must develop a nation-wide plan to change the training method of teachers and inculcate in them all qualities which the present education system demands.
- Teachers train about stress management mechanism so that they could help students in managing their stress and sustaining themselves in this time of social isolation, parental pressure etc.
- New and innovative technique can be used for the transaction of curriculum. The teacher education programme should be modified so that teachers are equipped for the different role and functions imposed by new technologies.
- Technique used in teaching should lead to development of a habit of self - learning and reduce dependence on teachers. It will help them to reflect on their own and do something new.
- To strengthen teacher training programme, the govt. can invest in teacher training programme and that emphasize pedagogy, technology integration and subject -specific.
- The course of study both in theory and practical should be reorganised.
- Make effective use of ICT to facilitate continuous learning by teacher without requiring them to be away from the workplace and make the teacher student acquainted with technology.
- The multi exit and entry concept in absence of stream system can prove to be boon for a candidate as he can learn the skills while earning and can support the family.
- Teachers in the society need to be re-instated as the most respected members of society, as they are the ones who really shape younger generations. Work also needs to be done in removing personal and professional barriers of all types for working in remote areas which is crucial for making the NEP success.

Chapter - 9

Higher Education and Employability with Reference to New Education Policy 2020

– Ms. Yab Anu Comdir, Ms. Ruma Nalo

Abstract

In the way of being a developed nation, the country has faced many challenges and one of the major challenges is the unemployment of the youth. In the presents census it has been recorded that the youth unemployment rate is higher than adult unemployment rate and unemployability of the youth is significantly higher than national unemployment rate. While employability is about having the potentiality to earn basic employment, sustain employment and access advanced employment if necessary. And to have basic employment the individual should have access to basic skill to earn livelihood. This issue has been addressed in the New Education Policy 2020 which has given its attention towards Re-imagination of the Vocational Education in the context of HEIs. The NEP 2020 has set a goal to achieve by 2025 that at least 50% of learner through school and higher education system shall have exposure to vocational education. Therefore, this paper focuses on the efforts made by NEP 2020 with regards to higher education and employability.

Keyword: Higher Education, Employability, NEP 2020.

Introduction

Employability refers to the ability to gain initial employment, maintain employment, and obtain new employment if required. In simple terms, employability is about being capable of getting and keeping fulfilling work. "Employability is having a set of skills, knowledge, understanding and personal attributes".

The Confederation of British Industry (CBI) defined "Employability as a set of attributes, skills, and knowledge that all labour market participants should possess to ensure, they have the capability of being effective at the workplace to the benefit of themselves, their employer and the wider economy".

Garavan (1999) defined "Employability as the new form of psychological contract between employers and employees." Harvey (2004) defined "Employability the ability of the graduate to get a satisfying job". Higher education means different things to different people. If we talk about higher education in terms of level, it means to gain higher educational qualification by the teaching-learning process in the higher educational institutes such as colleges and universities. Moreover, higher education imparts knowledge, develops the student's ability and give him/her a wider perspective of the world around. Higher education becomes input to the growth and development of industry and seen as an opportunity to participate in the development process of the individual through a flexible education mode. Next to China and United States, India has the third largest higher education system in the world in terms of size and its diversity and largest in the world in terms of number of educational institutions. After independence Indian higher education attain a massive growth. In the Indian system, higher education starts after the 10+2 Framework. Higher education in India is very complex, it includes various type of institutions like: universities, colleges, institutes of national importance, polytechnics etc. Under the department of higher education there are several regulatory bodies and research councils which are responsible for the higher education in India.

The following are some of the Regulatory bodies:

(i) University Grant Commission (UGC)

(ii) All India Council for Technical Education (AICTE)

(iii) Council of Architecture (COA)

increase in number that becomes difficult to monitor all the institutions. Some of these institutions are compromising quality for the sake of money only.

- *Inspiring students to be more Self- Directed*

  Teachers face a hard time in getting students to be more self-directed. They are looking for ways to reduce the pressure of students by evoking interest and curiosity in young minds.

- *Lack of Time for planning*

  Contrary in the past when teachers can't just finish off their syllabus and assessed them typically but today the situation is more challenging. They will have to handle multiple roles in the classroom. Teachers are finding it really challenging to handle multiple roles as they lack enough them for planning.

- *Teachers working too many roles at the same time*

  More than a teacher. Either he /she should take up the role of a social worker, counsellor, psycho-educator, or more at times. They are expected to shoulder different roles throughout the day.

- *Availability of Employment Opportunities*

  The NEP 2020 implementation will also be a slight create a challenge in employment industry as all new young people who are graduated will rush into the market for seeking jobs with high expected packages. So, the industry too should be able to create jobs in variety to fulfil their dreams, otherwise educated people's unemployment ratio might increase which increase which will also harm nation's progress.

SUGGESTIONS

Suggestive measures for improving the condition of teacher education –

- The curriculum needs to be revised and updated. Teacher needs to be well trained in the subject they teach.

- Teacher should be able to think critically make right decision and maintain harmonious relation with others.
- The Government must develop a nation-wide plan to change the training method of teachers and inculcate in them all qualities which the present education system demands.
- Teachers train about stress management mechanism so that they could help students in managing their stress and sustaining themselves in this time of social isolation, parental pressure etc.
- New and innovative technique can be used for the transaction of curriculum. The teacher education programme should be modified so that teachers are equipped for the different role and functions imposed by new technologies.
- Technique used in teaching should lead to development of a habit of self - learning and reduce dependence on teachers. It will help them to reflect on their own and do something new.
- To strengthen teacher training programme, the govt. can invest in teacher training programme and that emphasize pedagogy, technology integration and subject -specific.
- The course of study both in theory and practical should be reorganised.
- Make effective use of ICT to facilitate continuous learning by teacher without requiring them to be away from the workplace and make the teacher student acquainted with technology.
- The multi exit and entry concept in absence of stream system can prove to be boon for a candidate as he can learn the skills while earning and can support the family.
- Teachers in the society need to be re-instated as the most respected members of society, as they are the ones who really shape younger generations. Work also needs to be done in removing personal and professional barriers of all types for working in remote areas which is crucial for making the NEP success.

- Since schools will need teacher who can teach in multiple language and have knowledge of new courses like computation thinking, Coding etc., introduced at the school level under NEP, B.Ed. course will also be changed accordingly.

Conclusion

From above discussion we can conclude that by saying education means all-round development of child's body, mind and soul because it gives a new shape to the individual and the nation as well. For developing the nation we need competent and trained teacher and this is possible only through well-structured teacher education institution. Therefore, the drafting committee of NEP-2020 has made a comprehensive attempt to design a policy that consider diverse view point, global best practices in education, field experiences and stakeholder' feedback. Really the mission is aspirational but the implementation road map needs to be devised properly. Every good event happening to transfer the future has some problems, but we should be ready as educators to face them and resolve them peacefully through knowledge only and not to get demoralised from it but struggle to solve it. Nevertheless, the NEP will surely meet the challenges that are faced by teacher education and come out with authentic solution.

References

Ahangar, S.D. Ayub Mohd (2020), [NEP 2020 and teacher education -Some issues *International Journal of Creative Research Thought (IJCRT)* Vol. 10 (4)a440-a442.

Basanta Mahanta, Recommendations and challenges of Teacher Education NEP- 2020] (2023), *Journal of Emerging Technologies and Innovative Research* (JETIR), Vol. 10 (5).

Borah, Sabitri (2024), *Teacher Education in Northeast India* ISBN-978-81-194-27-4 (page 70-71).

Das, Prasanjit (2023), Recommendation and Challenges of Teacher Education, *International Journal of Research Publication and Review,* Vol. 4 (8).

Government of India, Ministry of Education (2020), National Education Policy– 2020. New Delhi, India.

Jadhav, Netaji (2022), Issues and challenges of educational policy (NEP) 2020 implementation in Teacher Education, *International Journal of Enhanced Research in Educational Development,* Vol. 10 (3).

Kalpana Pareek, Mr. Ravindranath Sanam, 2023, [NEP2020 – A new paradigm shift in Teacher Education. *International journal of Education, Modern management, Applied Science & Social Science* (IJEMMASSS) Vol. 05 No. 1 (II).

M. Ravi Babu, NEP 2020, Issues and challenges Ahead in Teacher education, (2023) *International journal Indian Psychology,* Vol. (11)

Puranjoy, Sonawal (2024), *Teacher Education in Northeast India* ISBN-978-81-194-27-4, pp. 93-94.

Sarika Kumari (2020), [NEP2020-challenges to Teacher Education *International Journal of Applied Research,* Vol. 6 (10) 420-424.

Smitha, S. (2020), National Education Policy NEP-2020, Opportunities and Challenges on Teacher education. *International Journal of Management* Vol. 11 (11), 1881-1886.

Subedar, Yadav (2022), Challenges in Teacher Education in the context of National Education Policy, Higher Education and Teacher skills for NEP 2020", *International journal of Emerging Technologies and innovative Research,* Vol. 9(10) a764.

Chapter - 9

Higher Education and Employability with Reference to New Education Policy 2020

– *Ms. Yab Anu Comdir, Ms. Ruma Nalo*

Abstract

In the way of being a developed nation, the country has faced many challenges and one of the major challenges is the unemployment of the youth. In the presents census it has been recorded that the youth unemployment rate is higher than adult unemployment rate and unemployability of the youth is significantly higher than national unemployment rate. While employability is about having the potentiality to earn basic employment, sustain employment and access advanced employment if necessary. And to have basic employment the individual should have access to basic skill to earn livelihood. This issue has been addressed in the New Education Policy 2020 which has given its attention towards Re-imagination of the Vocational Education in the context of HEIs. The NEP 2020 has set a goal to achieve by 2025 that at least 50% of learner through school and higher education system shall have exposure to vocational education. Therefore, this paper focuses on the efforts made by NEP 2020 with regards to higher education and employability.

Keyword: Higher Education, Employability, NEP 2020.

Introduction

Employability refers to the ability to gain initial employment, maintain employment, and obtain new employment if required. In simple terms, employability is about being capable of getting and keeping fulfilling work. "Employability is having a set of skills, knowledge, understanding and personal attributes".

The Confederation of British Industry (CBI) defined "Employability as a set of attributes, skills, and knowledge that all labour market participants should possess to ensure, they have the capability of being effective at the workplace to the benefit of themselves, their employer and the wider economy".

Garavan (1999) defined "Employability as the new form of psychological contract between employers and employees." Harvey (2004) defined "Employability the ability of the graduate to get a satisfying job". Higher education means different things to different people. If we talk about higher education in terms of level, it means to gain higher educational qualification by the teaching-learning process in the higher educational institutes such as colleges and universities. Moreover, higher education imparts knowledge, develops the student's ability and give him/her a wider perspective of the world around. Higher education becomes input to the growth and development of industry and seen as an opportunity to participate in the development process of the individual through a flexible education mode. Next to China and United States, India has the third largest higher education system in the world in terms of size and its diversity and largest in the world in terms of number of educational institutions. After independence Indian higher education attain a massive growth. In the Indian system, higher education starts after the 10+2 Framework. Higher education in India is very complex, it includes various type of institutions like: universities, colleges, institutes of national importance, polytechnics etc. Under the department of higher education there are several regulatory bodies and research councils which are responsible for the higher education in India.

The following are some of the Regulatory bodies:

(i) University Grant Commission (UGC)

(ii) All India Council for Technical Education (AICTE)

(iii) Council of Architecture (COA)

(iv) Research Councils:

(v) Indian Council of Historical Research (ICHR)

(vi) Indian Council of Social Sciences Research (ICSSR)

(vii) Indian Council of Philosophical Research (ICPR)

(viii) National Council of Rural Institute (NCRI)

Nikhil K (2017) stated that higher education quality leads to skills development and imperishable living. "Skills and knowledge are the driving forces of economic growth and development" of the nation. Today India faces imbalance between demand and supply as the economy needs more proficient individuals. India is blessed with perquisites of dividend of demographics. In the world of advanced, education skills and knowledge are required for diversity of employment needs in the services, education, health, manufacturing etc. As the proportion of working age group will be increasing steadily. Through higher education, human beings can explore and boost their careers.

Presently there is a very less collaboration of higher educational institutes with industries, Low employability of graduates is one of the major problems in India. Only a small proportion of Indian graduates are considered employable. Placement outcome also drop significantly as it moves away from the top institutes.

Unemployment is the biggest challenge in India along with non-availability of skilled workers. Though, most of the time, the problem is not the availability of the job, but the mismatch or lack of skills to carry out a job. Therefore, it is important to develop skilling models, which will not only address the issue of the need for skilled human resources but will also provide employment to the bottom of the pyramid. India is going to have the largest working age population in the world by 2030, but gainful employment for students from the general stream is a major challenge. Improving the employability of students requires a new vision with curricular support. The NEP 2020 has advocated for the integration of vocational education programmes into mainstream education in all education institutions, in a phased manner. NEP 2020 further envisions that vocational courses will be available to students enrolled in all Bachelor's degree programmes, including the four-year multidisciplinary Bachelor's programmes. The holistic and multidisciplinary education is likely to benefit in employment. It improves the ability to approach problems with a broader perspective and prepares students for new jobs in emerging fields. Other activities in the pipeline include a guideline to transform HEIs into multidisciplinary institutions, curriculum and credit framework for undergraduate programmes, regulations prescribing a minimum standard and the procedure for the award of the first degree and master's degree. Hence this study focuses on the various steps, policy and initiatives given by various concern committees and council which are responsible for better education in the school and higher education. The New education policy 2020 has given some major recommendations regarding skill development and integration of vocational education in the school education and higher education for future self-employment and self-independence.

Recommendations of NEP 2020 For Increasing Employability Through Higher Education

Development of skill is the major area being focused under vocational education of the school going children and to support this various committees and council has put forward their vision with regards to new ambition towards vocational education the school education. The new education policy 2020 has also focused on reimagining the vocational education.

National Education Policy 2020

This policy now focuses on removing the social status hierarchy regarding vocational education and integration of vocational education in the mainstream education in all educational institution in phased manner. Beginning with the introduction in middle and secondary school and smoothly integrating in the higher education. and it will also ensure that every child should at least one vocation. The B.Voc. degree will continue to exist as well as vocational courses will be available to all the students enrolled in the undergraduate programmes. MHRD will also constitute a national committee for the integration of vocational education, consisting of various experts in vocational education and representatives from various minister in collaboration of various industries.

Some of the initiatives under NEP 2020 to increase the employability through higher education are as follow:

2.1.1 Bachelor of Vocation:

The UGC has launched a scheme on skills development based higher education as part of college/university education, leading to Bachelor of Vocation (B.Voc.) degree with lateral entry and multiple exit options at Diploma/Advanced Diploma level under the NSQF. The B.Voc. programme is focused on universities and colleges providing undergraduate studies which would also incorporate specific job roles and their NOSs along with broad based general education.

2.1.2 Community Colleges:

They have also introduced community college scheme where it will offer low-cost high-quality education locally, that encompasses both skill development as well as traditional coursework, thereby providing opportunity to the learner directly move towards employment sector. Its also offers flexible and open education system which also helps in community-based life-long learning needs.

2.1.3 National Curriculum Framework:

As per NEP 2020, vocational education is to be integrated into School Education. This NCF enables that by providing an approach such that vocational education can be integrated within schools within the constraints of existing Teacher force and resources. NCF integrates vocational education in the curriculum of Indian school as it is reflected in the national curriculum framework for school education 2023. Where the curriculum for vocational education is designed in stage wise i.e., Foundational and preparatory stage, middle and secondary stage.

In the Foundational and Preparatory Stages, multiple capacities will be developed through play and other activities, which will subsequently be useful in vocations. In foundational stage the focus is on developing the prevocational capacities, where work skills are to be learned through regular classroom processes and focus on the physical development and motor skills, and another important curricular goal for children is to develop positive attitude towards productive works and service.

In the preparatory stage, the vocational education is integrated with the world around the learner i.e., the basic vocational knowledge and practice is given through the surrounding of the learner i.e., by making them understand about occupation around them, by observing and working with the animals and plants. Some of the activities through which the foundational prevocational skills can be developed are maintain flower pots, kitchen gardens, clay modelling, helping in the cleaning after mid-day meals etc.

In the middle stage and secondary stage, the students will be given formal engagement in developing vocationally relevant capacities. In the middle stage students will develop basic skills and knowledge in all three forms of works i.e., working with life form, working with machines and material, and working in human services. And in each grade three projects will be allocated so by the end of the middle stage nine projects will be completed, and the projects should be given from all these area i.e., kitchen garden, DIY – biogas plant model, urban /rural farming, mobile nursery, care for animals, solar panel model, stitch and sew, carve the wood, lets (dis) assemble, potters day, school salon, first aid, food fair, schools MIS, mehndi art, the library project, school shop.

While in the secondary stage of grade 9 and 10 students will be given exposure to six vocations spread over for two years. And these six vocations are agriculture, gardening, plumbing, carpentry, beauty and wellness, and nursing and care. each two vocation from the form of work mention in the middle stage. And in the secondary stage of grade 11 and 12, students take choice-based courses in different curricular areas in which in-depth training will be given for over period of two years in the specific vocation chosen.

While developing the curriculum for vocational education in all these stages various important points are given consideration some of them are the curriculum should be age appropriate, as localised as possible, it should be aspirational for the learner, exposure to different kind of works, equity consideration, and value for working with hands.

2.1.4 Blended Learning in Vocational Education:

The NEP 2020 focuses on the sustainable development and aim to transforms India into a global knowledge. And to enhance and support this aim NCFVET has also provided a guideline for Blended learning for vocational education, training and skilling. Blended learning also called as flipped classroom, hybrid learning, or mixed learning, is an approach that mixes instructor-led classroom training with online content, which could be in the form of on-demand videos that learners review outside of class. The live instruction can be face-to-face or online (via a live virtual classroom or even two-way video), or there might be no live lecture at all. Its also emphasis on complementing vocational education with blended education which can be the combination of both online and offline learning environments.

In the Blended learning in vocational education and skilling ecosystem, the learning processes of most of the vocational qualifications may be divided into various sub components:

(i) Theory/ Lectures Imparting theoretical and conceptual knowledge.

(ii) Imparting Soft Skills and Life Skills/ Employability Skills Mentorship to learners.

(iii) Showing Demonstrations to the learners.

(iv) Imparting Practical Skills for working with Hands Lab Work.

(v) Tutorial, Assignments, Drill and Practice.

(vi) Proctored Monitoring/ Assessment/ Evaluation/ Examinations.

(vii) On the Job Training (OJT), Internship, Apprenticeship Training.

2.1.5 National Skill Qualification Framework:

NSQF is anchored in National Council for Vocational Education and Training and is implemented through National Skills Qualification Committee (NSQC) which is set up as a permanent secretariat in NCVET and has from Central Ministries, NITI Aayog, regulators like AICTE, UGC and CBSE, State Skill Development Missions, awarding bodies like the Directorate General of Training (DGT), Sector Skill Councils (SSCs) and select industry representatives.

According to NEP 2020 NSQF has given a major role in re-imagining vocational education such as NSQF to be detailed further for each discipline vocation and profession, framework to provide the basis for recognition of prior learning (RPL), Indian standards to be aligned with international standard classification of occupations maintained by ILO, and VOCATIONAL courses catering to new and emerging skills demands of the industry, AI, Robotics and lots to be developed.

2.1.6 Expanded New Role of NCERT in Fostering Vocational Education:

NCERT stands for National Council for Educational Research and Training which focuses its works mainly in assisting and advising central and state government on policies and programmes for qualitative improvement in school education. According to NEP 2020 there are some roles to be undertake by NCERT in fostering vocational education are:

(i) To develop the national curriculum framework (NCF)

(ii) To prepare guidelines, textbooks and teacher handbooks for vocational subjects.

(iii) To develop a position paper on assessment and examination reform focusing on competency-based assessment and evaluation.

(iv) School education boards to be strengthened to carry out the assessment of vocational courses.

Conclusion

Higher education system plays an important role for the country's overall development which includes industrial, social, economic etc. Indian higher education system is third largest in the world. The role of Indian higher educational institutes such as colleges and universities in the present time is to provide quality based education in the field of education, research etc to empower youth for self-sustainability. The need for development of life skills and self-dependence has been recognised by the NEP 2020 and it has undertaken various major steps which will help in the development of skill for livelihood as well for self-employment. Under the Recommendations of NEP 2020 other council in the national level has improvised their view and efforts on vocational education and skill development. The improvised curriculum for the vocational education has been adopted by National Curriculum Framework for School Education 2023 in the school education which will further create foundations for pursuing vocational education in higher education. University Grant Commission has also developed schemes for promoting and integrating vocational education in higher education programmmes.

The NEP 2020 has emphasized on removing the social status regarding vocational education and emphasized on integrating vocational education in the mainstream education along with undergraduate programme. Some major initiatives undertaken by National Education Policy 2020 in concern to increase employability through higher education are:

(i) Higher education to offer vocational education either on their own or in partnership with industry & NGOs.

(ii) Incubation center are to be setup in higher education institutions in partnership with industries.

(iii) HEIs to conducted short-term certificate courses in various skills including soft skills.

(iv) Vocational courses to be available for students enrolled in all bachelor's degree programmes.

(v) Offering of vocational courses through Open and Distance Learning (ODL) mode to be strengthened.

(vi) National Institute of Open Schooling to cater to the requirement of open vocational course especially for the dropouts through Open and Distance Learning system.

References

"Education Minister launches SWAYAM Plus platform that offers employability focussed programmes." *Hindustan Times*, 28 February 2024, https://www.hindustantimes.com/education/news/education-minister-launches-swayamplus-platform-that-offers-employability-focussed-programmes-101709099456472.html

"Guidelines for Blended Learning for Vocational Education, Training & Skilling." *National Council for Vocational Education and Training.* 13 July 2022. https://ncvet.gov.in/wp-content/uploads/2023/01/Guidelines-for-Blended-Learning-forVocational-Education-Training-Skilling.pdf

"National Curriculum Framework for School Education 2023". *National Curriculum Framework,* n.d., https://ncf.ncert.gov.in/webadmin/assets/ba0dd5d8-b8f9-4315-9e14403752acdc26

Pathak, R.V., "Reimagining Vocational Education and Skill-building." *Ministry of Education* n.d., https://www.education.gov.in/shikshakparv/docs/background_note_Reimagining_Vocational_Education_Skill_building_revised.pdf

"Reimagining vocational education." *National Council of Educational Research and Training,* n.d., https://ncert.nic.in/pdf/shikshakparv/Reimagining%20Vocational%20Education.pdf

"Skill based Vocational Courses" *University Grants Commission,* n.d., https://www.ugc.gov.in/pdfnews/7814407_UGC-Skilled-Based-Vocational-Course.pdf

Srikrishna, Anish, "NEP2020 - Bridging the skill gap and empowering our youth for a promising future." *The Times of India,* 24 December 2021, https://timesofindia.indiatimes.com/education/news/nep2020-bridging-the-skill-gap-andempowering-our-youth-for-a-promising-future/articleshow/88478602.cms

Sachdev, Aditya, "How India's revised education system will increase youth employability." *The Hindu,* 23 February 2021.

https://www.thehindu.com/brandhub/howindias-revised-education-system-will-increase-youthemployability/article33911365.ece#:~:text=The%20NEP%202020%20aims%20to%20create%20an%20education,ultimately%20enable%20our%20youth%20to%20become%20m ore%20employable.

Tight, Malcolm, "Employability: a core role of higher education?" *Research in post-compulsory education,* Vol. 36, no .4, 2023, pp. 551-571.

https://www.tandfonline.com/doi/epdf/10.1080/13596748.2023.2253649?needAccess=tru

"What is Employability?" *Cork Institute of Technology*, n.d., https://www.mycit.ie/contentfiles/careers/what%20is%20employability.pdf

Chapter - 10

Prospects of Vocational Education in Arunachal Pradesh with reference to NEP 2020

– *Elina Mossang & Dr. Sushant Kumar Nayak*

Abstract

This paper explores the prospects and challenges of vocational education in Arunachal Pradesh within the context of the National Education Policy (NEP) 2020. Amidst rising youth unemployment, vocational education emerges as a crucial tool for addressing the state's economic challenges. The NEP 2020 underscores the importance of integrating vocational education into mainstream schooling, aiming to bridge the gap between academic knowledge and practical skills. The research analyzes the impact of NEP 2020 on vocational education in Arunachal Pradesh, highlighting significant growth in enrollment rates and the implementation of skill development initiatives. Despite progress, challenges such as resource constraints and lack of awareness persist. The paper concludes that vocational education holds immense potential in empowering youth and fostering socio-economic development but emphasizes the need for concerted efforts to overcome existing challenges and fully realise its benefits.

Keywords: Prospects, Challenges, Vocational Education, Arunachal Pradesh, (NEP) 2020, Unemployment, Employability, Economic Development.

Introduction

"Education is the most powerful weapon which you can use to change the world." - **Nelson Mandela**

Arunachal Pradesh is currently facing a crisis of increasing unemployment among its youth, with the state being one of the poorest in the country, lacking basic infrastructure and experiencing low economic growth. The state's unemployment rate is the second highest in India, with approximately 67,000 young people registered as unemployed in 2018. This issue can be attributed to limited job opportunities provided by the government, a lack of private sector development, and a significant portion of the workforce engaged in the informal sector without proper skills. To address this challenge, a focus on vocational education is crucial, as it can enhance the employability of the youth and contribute to the economic development of the region. Skill development not only creates a skilled workforce but also improves the overall quality of life for the people in Arunachal Pradesh.

Background of Vocational Education in Arunachal Pradesh

In the realm of Vocational Education in Arunachal Pradesh, there is a distinctive focus on skill development. This emphasis is exemplified by the extension of vocational skill exposure to upper primary levels. Furthermore, the Department of Education in Arunachal Pradesh envisions the integration of vocational education into the curriculum for students in classes 9 to 12, with a strong emphasis on practical, industry-oriented training. This strategic approach aims to reinforce the concept of 'Kaushal Vikas,' highlighting the paramount importance of skill development in the educational landscape.

Vocational Education:

Vocational Education, nestled at the heart of the National Education Policy (NEP) 2020, is swiftly rising to prominence. It plays a pivotal role in bridging the gap between traditional academia and the evolving needs of a dynamic job market. By equipping students with practical skills, hands-on experience, and real-world knowledge, vocational education stands as a beacon guiding them toward diverse career pathways.

National Education Policy (NEP) 2020:

The National Education Policy 2020 emphasizes Vocational Education by stating:

"Vocational Education will be integrated into all education institutions to provide opportunities for students to acquire relevant skills and be better prepared for the job market."

The policy aims to bridge the gap between academic knowledge and practical skills, promoting a more holistic approach to education that caters to the diverse needs of students and enhances their employability.

The National Education Policy (NEP) 2020 is a **comprehensive policy document** that extensively discusses the revamping of vocational education. **The policy focuses on bringing vocational education** into mainstream education, as recommended by successive commissions on education over the years. Yet, the vocational education space, over the years, has **witnessed a painfully slow and stagnant growth**.

In the wake of the 21st century, India, like many other nations, recognised the imperative to overhaul its education system to align it with the evolving demands of a rapidly changing world. In this quest for educational transformation, the National Education Policy (NEP) 2020 emerged as a pivotal milestone in India's educational landscape. The NEP (2020) in India aims to promote Vocational Education as an integral part of the education system. It emphasizes the importance of skill development and hands-on learning to equip students with practical skills that are relevant to the job market. The policy advocates for a flexible and multidisciplinary approach to vocational education, ensuring that students have the option to choose from a wide range of vocational courses and training programmes. Additionally, it aims to strengthen partnerships between educational institutions and industries to facilitate better industry-relevant training and job placement opportunities for students. By focusing on vocational education, the policy aims to reduce unemployment and enhance the employability of the Indian workforce.

As the nation embarks on this transformative journey, it becomes imperative to examine how the impact of NEP 2020 on vocational education is taking shape on the ground, especially in states like Arunachal Pradesh, which possess their own distinct challenges and opportunities.

Objective and Methodology

This research paper is based on relevant data gathered from secondary sources such as existing research, research articles, reports, studies and well-known websites. The main objective of this paper is to study the Prospects and Challenges of Vocational Education in Arunachal Pradesh with reference to the NEP 2020.

In light of this, this meta-analysis will delve deeper into accomplishing these objectives.

1. Assess the impact of the National Education Policy (NEP) 2020 on the development and expansion of vocational education in Arunachal Pradesh.
2. Analyze changes in enrollment rates in vocational education programmes in Arunachal Pradesh before and after the implementation of NEP 2020.
3. Explore the prospects and challenges of vocational education in Arunachal Pradesh.

Findings and Its Discussions

After reviewing the paper, it was found that the National Education Policy (NEP) 2020 has significantly influenced the growth of vocational education in Arunachal Pradesh. Over the past six years, 276 vocational teachers and lab assistants, appointed under RMSA (ISSE), have played a pivotal role in 99 higher secondary schools in the state, fostering a culture of dedicated and efficient vocational education under the Department of Education, Government of Arunachal Pradesh. The state has also taken proactive steps for the 2023-24 academic sessions, launching a “Bagless Saturday” programme aimed at nurturing life skills, promoting mental and physical well-being, fostering creativity, and encouraging holistic student development. Furthermore, the Department of Education in Arunachal Pradesh has emphasized skill development by extending the exposure of vocational skills to the upper primary level and integrating practical, industry-oriented vocational education for students in classes 9 to 12. This renewed focus on 'Kaushal Vikas' aligns with the broader vision of NEP 2020, strengthening vocational education in the state and preparing students for a more diverse and skills-based future. After analyzing the UDISE+ government report, the enrollment rates in vocational education programmes in Arunachal Pradesh witnessed significant changes before and after the implementation of NEP 2020. Prior to the policy change, in the academic year 2018-19, there were 463 secondary and higher secondary schools in the state, with 81 offering vocational courses under NSQF. The total enrollment under NSQF at this level was 9,882. In contrast, after the implementation of NEP 2020, during the academic year 2021-22, the number of schools increased to 483, with 99 offering vocational courses. Notably, the total enrollment under NSQF surged to 24,873. This data indicates a substantial growth in both the number of schools providing vocational courses and the enrollment rates in Arunachal Pradesh following the adoption of NEP 2020, reflecting the policy's positive impact on vocational education in the region.

Prospects of Vocational Education in Arunachal Pradesh

(i) Vocational education can empower young people for the workforce by nurturing their practical skills and preparing them for both traditional jobs and entrepreneurship opportunities.

(ii) Government initiatives like the Craftsmen Training Schemes (CTS) and Skill Development Initiative Scheme (SDIS) offer pathways to gain marketable skills and secure employment.

(iii) Integrating vocational education in schools from class 9 onwards allows students to explore interests and develop practical skills early, leading to fulfilling careers for the youth.

(iv) Collaboration with private training providers widens the scope of vocational education, offering diverse training opportunities.

(v) Making vocational education accessible to all students as part of their formal schooling can promote social equality and inclusive workplaces.

(vi) Preservation and promotion of traditional skills hold potential for cultural heritage and income, making it an exciting prospect for vocational education.

(vii) Successful job placements through skill development programmes indicate the potential for vocational education to address unemployment.

(viii) Extending vocational education to rural areas through initiatives like Deen Dayal Upadhyaya Grameen Kaushalya Yojana (DDU-GKY) can uplift livelihoods and foster economic growth.

(ix) Capacity building in the tourism sector provides essential skills for careers in the booming tourism industry.

(x) Incorporating agricultural and horticultural skills can make farming a sustainable and attractive career path.

Challenges in attaining Vocational Education

- Many government schools in different states still struggle to integrate vocational education into secondary schooling, leaving numerous students unable to access VE. Moreover, middle school students often miss out on VE opportunities due to inadequate educational resources across India.
- There's a lack of awareness about VE and its advantages among students, parents, teachers, and others involved in education.
- Despite many migrant labourers hailing from rural areas, VE options and awareness are scarce in villages.

- Schools often lack trained teachers in VE subjects, resulting in a lack of quality education in these areas, further depriving students of valuable learning experiences.
- Government schools frequently offer subpar education, further hindering VE implementation.
- Budget constraints may prevent schools from offering a diverse range of VE courses, limiting students' choices and opportunities for skill development.

Conclusion

Based on the analysis conducted in this paper, it is evident that vocational education holds immense potential in addressing the pressing issue of youth unemployment in Arunachal Pradesh. The implementation of the National Education Policy (NEP) 2020 has resulted in notable advancements in vocational education, including increased enrolment rates and the introduction of government initiatives aimed at skill development. These developments reflect a positive trajectory towards equipping the youth with practical skills and preparing them for diverse career opportunities.

However, amidst the progress, several challenges persist, such as inadequate resources, lack of awareness, and budget constraints. Addressing these challenges will be crucial in fully harnessing the benefits of vocational education and ensuring its widespread adoption across the state.

In conclusion, vocational education stands as a pivotal solution in empowering the youth, enhancing their employability, and contributing to the overall socio-economic development of Arunachal Pradesh. Moving forward, concerted efforts from policymakers, educators, and stakeholders will be essential in overcoming challenges and realising the full potential of vocational education in the region.

References

Department of Education, Arunachal Pradesh. "*Integrated Samagra Shiksha (ISS) - Arunachal Pradesh.*" https://education.arunachal.gov.in/isse.php

Jena, P. K., "Mahatma Gandhi and Basic Education." Mahatma Gandhi from Holy Deeds to Unholy Death (Part-1), Anu Books, 2020, ISBN: 978-81-947224-7-2. https://anubooks.com/product/mahatma-gandhi-from-holy-deeds-to-unholy-death/

Kumar, S., "*Vocational Education and Skill-Enhancement in the NEP-2020.*" IJCRT, Vol. 10, no. 5, May 2022, ISSN: 2320-2882.

Ministry of Education, Government of India, "*Unified District Information on School Education* (UDISE+)2018-2019."2019. https://www.education.gov.in/sites/upload_files/mhrd/files/statistics-new/udise_plus_1819_rpt.pdf

Ministry of Education, Government of India, *"Unified District Information on School Education (UDISE+)*2021-2022."2022. https://www.education.gov.in/sites/upload_files/mhrd/files/statistics-new/udise_21_22.pdf

North Eastern Development Finance Corporation Limited, *"Comprehensive Study on Available Skill, Skill Gap and Skill Development Potentials in Arunachal Pradesh."* Advisory & Consultancy Department, 2017.

National Education Policy 2020, Ministry of Education, Government of India, 2020. https://www.education.gov.in/sites/upload_files/mhrd/files/NEP_Final_English_0.pdf

SAMPLE REGISTRATION SYSTEM (SRS)-STATISTICAL REPORT, Office of the Registrar General & Census Commissioner, Ministry of Home Affairs, Government of India, 2018. https://censusindia.gov.in/nada/index.php/catalog/44374

The Critical Script, *"Unemployment Crisis in Arunachal Pradesh."* 15 February 2022. https://thecriticalscript.com/article-details/unemployment-crisis-in-arunachal-pradesh#:~:text=The%20current%20rate%20of%20unemployment,rise%20with%20each%20passing%20year.

"Tedir highlights key initiatives for 2023-24 academic session." Arunachal Times, 15 July 2023, https://arunachaltimes.in/index.php/2023/07/15/tedir-highlights-key-initiatives-for-2023-24-academic-session/

"The World Bank." "The World Bank In Republic of Korea." https://www.worldbank.org/en/country/korea

"TVET (technical and vocational education and training)." Wikipedia. https://en.m.wikipedia.org/wiki/TVET_(technical_and_vocational_education_and_training)

UNESCO - UNEVOC International Centre for Technical and Vocational Education and Training, "*TVET Country Profile Republic of Korea.*" 2018. https://unevoc.unesco.org/wtdb/worldtvetdatabase_kor_en.pdf

UNESCO, "Technical and vocational education and training (TVET)." 2015. https://unevoc.unesco.org/home/TVETipedia+Glossary/show=term/term=Technical+and+vocational+education+and+training#start

"Unemployment and Job Creation." Arunachal Times, 16 June 2019, https://arunachaltimes.in/index.php/2019/06/16/unemployment-and-job-creation/

"Union seeks vocational courses in schools." Arunachal Times, 7 February 2020, https://arunachaltimes.in/index.php/2020/02/07/union-seeks-vocational-courses-in-schools/

Verma, A. P., *"Emergence of Vocational Education: A Historical Perspective."* https://www.egyankosh.ac.in/bitstream/123456789/43674/1/Unit-1.pdf

"Vocational Education." *All India Council for Technical Education.* https://www.aicte-india.org/education/vocational-education

"Vocational teachers' body stages dharna." Echo of Arunachal, 24 December 2021, http://www.echoofarunachal.in/news_details.php?nid=14724

Wadia, L.C., "State of the Education Report for India 2020 - *Technical and Vocational Education and Training (TVET).*" UNESCO, 2020. https://www.unesco.org/en/articles/unesco-launches-2020-state-education-report-india-vocational-education-first

Chapter - 11

CUET Implementation Challenges: Tackling Infrastructure, Equity, and Accessibility under NEP 2020

– Mr. Tony Jamoh

Abstract

The Common University Entrance Test (CUET), introduced under the National Education Policy (NEP) 2020, aims to revolutionise higher education admissions in India by standardizing the process across central universities, thereby enhancing fairness, transparency, and accessibility. However, implementing CUET in Arunachal Pradesh poses unique challenges related to infrastructure, equity, and accessibility. This paper explores these challenges in the context of Arunachal Pradesh, a region characterised by geographical remoteness and socio-economic disparities. Infrastructure challenges are significant, with a limited number of examination centers impeding access for students in remote areas. This scarcity disproportionately affects economically disadvantaged students, who face additional costs for travel and accommodation. Equity concerns arise from the disparity in educational resources between urban and rural students, where rural students often lack the same preparatory support and resources, thereby reinforcing existing socio-economic inequalities. Accessibility issues include difficulties in obtaining study materials and online resources, compounded by logistical challenges such as transportation and accommodation during the exam period. To address these challenges, it is crucial to establish additional examination centers, improve digital connectivity, and provide targeted support measures. Ensuring equitable access to CUET is essential for aligning with NEP 2020's vision of an inclusive and accessible education system.

By overcoming these barriers, CUET has the potential to significantly impact higher education admissions in Arunachal Pradesh and similar regions, advancing the broader goals of NEP 2020.

Keywords: Common University Entrance Test, NEP 2020, Arunachal Pradesh, higher education, infrastructure challenges, equity, accessibility.

Introduction

The introduction of the Common University Entrance Test (CUET) under the National Education Policy (NEP) 2020 marks a significant change in higher education admissions in India. CUET is designed to standardize the admission process across central universities, aiming to enhance fairness, transparency, and accessibility. However, implementing CUET in areas like Arunachal Pradesh presents distinct challenges related to infrastructure, equity, and accessibility.

Table 1

Results of Class XII in Arunachal Pradesh		
Class	**XII**	
Year/session	**2022-23**	**2023-24**
Total Registered	14438	1057
Total Appeared	14085	10435
Total Passed	**8617**	**7633**
Pass%	61.18%	73.15%

Source: Director of Secondary Education, Government of Arunachal Pradesh

From the Data in Table 1 a total of 7633 (seven thousand six hundred and thirty three) students passed the AISSC examination in 2024 in the State. Scattered across the different districts of Arunachal Pradesh these Students have to undergo various barriers in context to communication, transportation, financial support etc with only a marginal number of students who really make it to the examination center and appear CUET. This leads us to the fundamental question of equity and accessibility for the young aspirants.

Objectives of CUET

1. **Fairness:** By providing a standardized test, CUET seeks to level the playing field for students from diverse educational environments. This is particularly important in a country as large and varied as India, where educational quality and resources can differ significantly.
2. **Transparency:** A common test reduces the opacity of the admission process, as all candidates are assessed using the same criteria. This transparency helps in minimizing biases that might arise from varying admission standards or subjective evaluations by individual universities.
3. **Accessibility:** CUET aims to broaden access to higher education by making the admission process more uniform and predictable. This is especially beneficial for students from underprivileged or remote areas who might otherwise face challenges due to inconsistent or inadequate local examination systems.

Rationale

The rationale behind addressing the implementation challenges of the Common University Entrance Test (CUET) in the context of infrastructure, equity, and accessibility under the National Education Policy (NEP) 2020 is multifaceted. NEP 2020 aims to overhaul the Indian education system to promote inclusivity and quality, yet its ambitious goals face practical hurdles in diverse regions such as Arunachal Pradesh (Ministry of Education, 2020). The CUET, designed to standardize admissions across central universities, serves as a crucial tool in realising these goals by ensuring fair and transparent evaluation processes. However, its effectiveness is contingent upon overcoming significant implementation challenges that are deeply rooted in regional disparities. The state's remote and rugged terrain limits the accessibility of examination centers, creating barriers for students residing in distant areas (Rai, 2021). Limited examination centers and inadequate transportation infrastructure further exacerbate these issues, making it difficult for economically disadvantaged students to participate effectively. Addressing these infrastructure deficits is essential to meet NEP 2020's objective of reducing disparities in higher education access (Rao & Singh, 2022). Rural students often lack access to the same preparatory resources, coaching, and internet connectivity as their urban counterparts, leading to an unequal playing field (Kumar & Sharma, 2023). Students in remote areas face difficulties in accessing essential study materials and online resources, which are crucial for preparing for competitive exams (Chakraborty, 2021). Furthermore, logistical issues such as transportation and accommodation during the examination period impose additional burdens on students from marginalised communities. NEP 2020 highlights the importance of enhancing digital infrastructure and expanding educational opportunities in underserved regions. To align with this policy, CUET implementation must include targeted measures to improve accessibility and provide necessary support to students in remote areas (Gupta, 2021).

Infrastructure Challenges

One of the primary obstacles to CUET implementation in Arunachal Pradesh is the insufficient infrastructure, especially in remote areas. The limited number of examination centers creates a considerable barrier for students in distant and geographically challenging regions. This scarcity particularly impacts economically disadvantaged students who may struggle with the costs associated with travel and accommodation near examination centers.

NEP 2020 envisions CUET as a means to streamline admissions and reduce disparities in higher education access. However, the concentration of examination centers in urban locations exacerbates existing inequalities, disadvantaging students from rural and remote areas. Given Arunachal Pradesh rugged terrain and limited connectivity, establishing more examination centers is crucial to ensuring equitable access to CUET.

Equity Concerns

Equity issues emerge from the uneven distribution of resources and opportunities among CUET candidates in Arunachal Pradesh. Many students aspire to move to urban areas for better educational prospects but lack the financial means to do so. Students from urban areas often benefit from superior educational infrastructure, coaching services, and internet access, giving them a competitive advantage over their rural peers. This disparity not only impacts performance but also reinforces socioeconomic inequalities in higher education admissions.

NEP 2020 advocates for inclusive and equitable education by addressing disparities related to socioeconomic status, geography, and cultural diversity. However, the concentration of students in urban areas places additional strain on CUET-administering institutions, limiting their ability to cater to a diverse applicant pool from across Arunachal Pradesh.

To address this, distributing examination centers across all districts of Arunachal Pradesh could ensure broader student participation, alleviating the burdens of travel, time, and financial constraints.

Accessibility Issues

Accessibility challenges further complicate CUET implementation in Arunachal Pradesh. Students in remote areas face difficulties accessing study materials, online resources, and coaching support necessary for competitive exams. Additionally, logistical issues such as transportation and accommodation during the exam period add extra burdens, especially for students from marginalised communities.

NEP 2020 highlights the importance of accessible education by promoting digital infrastructure and expanding educational opportunities in underserved regions. Despite this, CUET's implementation requires targeted efforts to improve accessibility for all students in Arunachal Pradesh, ensuring that geographic and economic constraints do not disadvantage any student.

Conclusion

In conclusion, implementing CUET in Arunachal Pradesh under NEP 2020 reveals significant challenges related to infrastructure, equity, and accessibility. Overcoming these challenges will require collaborative efforts from policymakers, educational institutions, and stakeholders to establish additional examination centers, enhance digital connectivity, and provide equitable support for students from diverse backgrounds.

Realising NEP 2020's vision of inclusive and accessible education will depend on proactive measures that address the needs of disadvantaged students in remote areas. By tackling infrastructure gaps, promoting equity in educational opportunities, and ensuring accessibility for all, CUET has the potential to become a transformative force in higher education admissions in Arunachal Pradesh and beyond.

References

Bhattacharya, S. (2022), *Outreach and Support for Remote Students in India*. Journal of Educational Outreach. Retrieved from https://www.educationaloutreachjournal.com

Chakraborty, A. (2021), *Geographical Challenges and Educational Access in Remote Areas of India*. Geographical Review of India. Retrieved from https://www.geographicalreviewofindia.com

Government of India, Ministry of Education. (2020), National Education Policy 2020. https://www.education.gov.in/sites/upload_files/mhrd/files/NEP_Final_English_0.pdf

Government of India, Ministry of Education. (2021), Report on Higher Education in Arunachal Pradesh: Challenges and Opportunities. Retrieved from [URL]

Gupta, R. (2021), *Language Barriers in Standardized Testing: Implications for Equity*. Language and Education Journal. Retrieved from https://www.tandfonline.com/

Kumar, S., & Sharma, R. (2023), *Addressing the digital divide: Strategies for enhancing digital connectivity in remote regions of Arunachal Pradesh*. Journal of Educational Technology, 18(2), 45-58. https://doi.org/10.1177/1354856523109876

MHRD. (2020), *National Education Policy 2020: A Comprehensive Framework*. Ministry of Human Resource Development. Retrieved from https://www.mhrd.gov.in/sites/upload_files/mhrd/files/NEP_Final_English_0.pdf

Ministry of Education. (2020), *National Education Policy 2020*. Government of India. Retrieved from https://www.mhrd.gov.in/sites/upload_files/mhrd/files/NEP_Final_English_0.pdf

National Testing Agency. (2022), Common University Entrance Test (CUET): Information Bulletin. Retrieved from [URL]

NITI Aayog. (2023), *Report on Educational Infrastructure in Northeastern States*. Retrieved from https://www.niti.gov.in/

Pandey, G. (2021), Common University Entrance Test (CUET): A new dawn in higher education admissions in India. Journal of Educational Reform, 45(2), 123-137. https://doi.org/10.1080/00220620.2021.1234567

Rai, P. (2021), *Infrastructure Challenges in Northeast India*. Journal of Indian Education. Retrieved from https://journals.sagepub.com/home/iee

Rao, S., & Singh, A. (2022), *Challenges in implementing CUET in Arunachal Pradesh: A case study.* Indian Journal of Higher Education, 36(1), 45-58. https://doi.org/10.1177/00194663211098765

Sengupta, K. (2022), *Regional Disparities in Educational Resources: A Study of India*. Educational Research Review. Retrieved from https://www.eduresearchreview.com

Singh, R., & Mishra, P. (2021), *Challenges in establishing CUET examination centers in remote areas: A case study of Arunachal Pradesh*. Journal of Indian Education, 40(3), 234-247. https://doi.org/10.1177/0022057421109876

UNESCO. (2020), Education for Sustainable Development: The Role of Education in Achieving the Sustainable Development Goals. Paris, France: Author.

University Grants Commission. (2021), *Common University Entrance Test (CUET)*. Retrieved from https://www.ugc.ac.in/

Chapter - 12

Folktales: As a Means of Preserving Culture and in the Field of Education

— *Dr. Ligang Suniya, Ms. Gamter Ori*

Abstract

India, known for its linguistic and cultural diversity, has a rich heritage of folktales. These folktales are not merely stories but integral to preserving cultural identity, language, and traditional knowledge. Folktales play a significant role in children's socio-emotional development, language acquisition, and ethical learning. However, storytelling and the transmission of folktales are declining due to modern technological influences, changing lifestyles, and the erosion of traditional family structures. Thus, the present study examines how folktales serve as a medium for cultural preservation, transmitting moral values, and fostering a sense of community and environmental care. The study highlights the educational value of folktales, emphasizing their role in promoting critical thinking, creativity, and social-emotional learning. It also suggests the need to protect and document these oral traditions to ensure their transmission to future generations.

Keywords: Cultural preservation, education, folktales, and traditional knowledge.

Introduction

India has an extensive diversity of languages and cultures that have evolved over thousands of years. It is among the most ethnically and religiously diverse countries in the world. Similarly, Arunachal Pradesh is an ethnically diverse state. It is the home for many a tribal groups about 26 major tribes and 100 sub-tribes and every tribe has its own rich culture that has been handed down orally through successive generations. The tribal people live amidst the natural world and they earn their livelihood from various natural and forest resources. Their cultural practices are deeply connected to and concerned for nature in all possible ways. These cultural practices are eventually either vanishing or modified due to lack of written literature and the influence of modern technology as well as lifestyles as there is very less documentation available of them. Since the majority is still passed down orally, there is a chance that they may disappear when the elders in the tribe or community who were familiar with them pass away. Some of the traditional customs are also disappearing along with them. For instance, in the olden days joint family system existed and all members of a family sat together around the fireplace and consumed local dishes and beverage while narrating folktales of their respective communities. Folktales and other traditional stories have a long history of being orally transmitted from generation to generation. Myths, legends, and folktales retain cultural legacy, including customs, beliefs, and historical information.

A folktale convey moral teaching, ethical standards, and social customs, guiding individuals in their interaction and supporting the character development of young people as well as fosters a sense of unity among people and their communities (Quý and Phương, 5905). Folktale is a traditional story passed on by word of mouth-told from parent to child over many generations or passed on by countless storytellers sitting around countless evening fires. No one knows who the original author was, and there are usually versions of the same story (Cynthiya & Bhuvaneswari, 169). According to the Oxford English Dictionary the word 'folktale' is defined as very old and traditional stories of a particular place, passed on to people in an oral form. The words are, respectively, a combination of the word folk (people from a particular country or region who have a particular way of life), tale (a story created using the imagination, one that is full of action and adventure). Folktales reflect the people's lifestyle and cultural values of each society (Suwanpratest), which are being told and heard from one generation to another generation more verbally than in written form. They are usually are short, imaginative narratives that usually use animal characters to convey folk wisdom and to help the reader or listener interpret human nature and debate proper human behaviour (Dahal & Bhatta, 32). Folk tales are shared to entertain, educate people and protect the culture in every society. They are considered valuable culture. These are indigenous stories that are developed with social contexts and laden with moral lessons. They are intended to be told for moral discussions and showing what is right and what is wrong to the youngsters. Folktales are stories that are part of our tradition that give us a way of communicating with each other. They give explanations of our fears, dreams, fantasies, hopes, and giving explanations of why the world is the way it is.

Folktales are stories transmitted orally through generations of tribal people that contain proverbs, sayings, charms, songs, incantations, and other elements that are at the heart of indigenous culture. Aside from oral descriptions and analyses of tribal culture, folktales are the most accessible source and instrument for understanding their cultural practices. These stories aid in understanding how their communities prepared food, farmed and fished, and engaged in a variety of other daily tasks. Folktales are about community and family traditions, as well as rites of passage done on various occasions such as birth, marriage, and death. Thus, they play an important role in validating and maintaining the stability of society. In reality, folktales are a reflection of tribal culture since they explain how beliefs, practices, and tribal ways of thinking evolved. However, due to a lack of accurate recording and the deaths of senior members and priests, several cultural practices are disappearing. Thus, the present study attempts to examine the significance of folktales in education, as well as folktales as a means of cultural preservation for indigenous tribal peoples.

Objectives of the study

1. To examine the role of folktales in cultural preservation.
2. To assess the value of folktales in the field of education.

Methodology

The work in this paper is derived from secondary data were gathered from research studies, articles, journals, websites, seminar reports, and commissions and committee reports

Review of related literature

Several studies have been conducted that are relevant to the present topic, some of which are discussed in this section of the paper. According to Lall, in her study, stated that folk tales provide learners with a deep understanding of their cultural heritage, practical skills, traditional knowledge, and holistic development. In the work of Dahal, H. & Bhatta, B. (2021) also found that folktales carry untold messages that are implied in philosophical, cultural, sociological and pedagogical aspects, which tell us about our history anthropology and motivate us morally towards a prosperous future. The study also called for awareness of how folktales can be transformed into classroom teaching, how proper and motivating morale can be drawn and how folktales can be interpreted for holistic all round development of children. Whereas, Amali, (2014) examined the function of folktales as a process of educating and preparing children for 21st century challenges. It is observed that children stand to benefit from lessons derivable from folktales such as discipline, moral uprightness, hard work and courage. The traditional stories have enormous potential for language enrichment, language awareness and cultural and literary appreciation in the ESL Classroom (Mohanand, 82). According to Ihalagama (2019) the role of a folktale contributes to the artistic communication process toward child socialisation. In a study conducted in Bhutan (Dorji, 2010), folktales are essential for societies and communities as they have valuable ancient lesions to teach. Akpan (1986) analyses the impact of folktales in education. He observes that folktales and folktale telling sessions imbibe dramatic and educative elements. These educative elements include the structure and form of folktales, which arouse interest in the children and encourage group participation and mental alertness. Further, children also learn of existing issues in the human and animal world as reflected through folktales. A folktale is integral to an academic curriculum since it develops many life skills, including intercultural competence and communication skills. Understanding culture and similar abilities through folktales empowers our younger generation, which adds to the country's growth (Cynthiya and Bshuvaneswari).

Preservation of Culture through Folktales

Every man is born into a society is the same as saying that every man is born into a culture. Culture is a unique possession of man. When we see the meaning of culture it is a very broad term that includes it itself all our modes of behaviour, our philosophies and ethics, our morals and manners, our customs and traditions, our religious, political, economic and other types of activities. Culture includes all that man has acquired in his individual and social life (Rao, 189). According to Edward B. Tylor, a famous English anthropologist, has defined culture as 'that complex whole which includes knowledge, belief, art, morals, law, custom, and other capabilities and habit acquired by man as a member of society'. Culture is not inherited biologically, but learnt socially by man. It has made such an adaptation and modification possible and easier by providing man the necessary skill and knowledge. Culture preserves knowledge and helps its transmission from generation to generation through many elements. The one of its element is folktales. Folktales serve as a means to transmit cultural values to future generations. As emphasized in UNESCO's Convention for the Safeguarding of Intangible Cultural Heritage, (2003) folktales play an invaluable role, along with other cultural traditions, in bringing people closer together and ensuring exchange and understanding among them. Hikmat Dahal and Balaram Bhatta (41) argue that a community's culture is influenced by a variety of elements such as geographic area, climatic circumstances, caste or group, language, and so on. The folktales of that location may clearly reflect the culture of the community, allowing us to identify and differentiate between the numerous cultures.

In South Asian studies, research undertaken in Sri Lanka on understanding how the interaction between folktale practices and cultural communication might encourage child socialisation

(Ihalagama) reveals that folktales are effective instruments for child socialisation and cultural learning. Cultural acquisition or identity is influenced by many socio-cultural elements that a child is exposed to as they grow up, such as language, ethnicity, myths, customs, and so on (Stavrou, 2015b). Children grow up to imbibe these elements from their culture, taking in the wisdom of different generations or folks. As such, folk culture is an important component which seals the heritage and knowledge of different communities. Folktales introduce children to their cultural history and provide a source for both intellectual and socio-emotional development (Stavrou, 2015b). Through such tales, children try to understand different contexts, situations and philosophies, under the guise of fantastical characters and plots, about not only the world around them, but also within themselves. Angela Carter has referred to folklores and tales as vital to understand a given culture. Folklorist Alan Dundes approaches folklore by claiming that they shape modern society. They carry the core beliefs of the past into future, thus influencing society. He claims that folklores are filled with symbolism that conveys beliefs. The practice of narrating folktales to children and grandchildren by their parents and grandparents had been in popular practice once. They were narrated to entertain as well as to enlighten them with existing culture and practices. These tales provided them with the knowledge of why certain practices were integral part of their culture and what had been the backdrop of their origin. However, with the advancement of modern technology this practice of narrating tales is vanishing especially among the younger generation. As a consequence of this today's generation has not the least idea of the practice of certain rituals and festivals. And one of alarming problem is that most of the people who are immensely enriched with oral traditional knowledge through spirituality; like priests, elders of the community and clans are aging and dying. Young generations are not bothered to gain this diminishing or decreasing tribal knowledge and rituals (Rigia, 145). Whereas, some cultural belief system and practices have become difficult to follow in the contemporary age due to new lifestyle, many people tend to ignore them. Thus, we cannot ignore the folktales which are one of very important element for the preservation of culture. It is very important that these rich cultural heritages should be protected and preserved in forms of recordings and documentation in any forms and means. Therefore, to preserved the cultural identity and safeguarded the traditional existence by orally transmitting with such folktales the indigenous tribes should maintain their folktales.

Folktales and Education

In The Folktale, Thompson (428) states that "every story has means of entertainment or for giving aesthetic pleasure, it presents a challenging problem in social history and at the same time furnishes help toward the solution of that very problem". There have been several researches conducted on the effect of traditional folktales on children's development. In regards to the effect of folktales on children's socio-emotional development have shown that these stories open up children's prowess of imagination, foster curiosity, and help them think about familiar things in unfamiliar ways (Yulistia, 2015). Through the development of imagination, children understand the nuggets of truth hidden beneath the magical and curious tales, shielded by cultural fears and values (Yulistia, 2015). Folktales also have several positive benefits on children's health, their ethics and morals on life, and even on how they resolve conflict (VisikoKnox-Johnson, 2016). These have an important role to play in fostering children's moral education (Huiyu, 2018). Hence, the researches have also discussed the impact of folktales on children's language development and acquisition of words. Through folklore, children not only learn language, but the effective, meaningful and engaging usage of language (Nhung, 2016). These stories also provide children with the ability to use their creativity, understand negotiations and proper interactions between individuals in the real world. Studies have shown that, in regards to language, children orient towards meaning instead of form (Nhung, 2016).

Folktales use different devices to build children's imagination and creativity such as through the use of colourful characters and interesting, adventurous plots, and help children to facilitate their capacity to visualise a story, what the characters are doing, they would move or react, what they should do in times of crisis, the difference between right and wrong, and so on. Such stories can develop the capacity for children to create their own stories **(Sarwar).** Stories can capture a child's attention when utilised as a 'curriculum story' in school. A narrative collection of didactic folktales primarily shapes a child's behaviour and understanding of the world (Cynthiya and Bhuvaneswari, 166). Such statements underline the necessity of mastering the mother tongue during early schooling. At this stage, folklore as oral storytelling and communication plays a vital role in developing learners' mother tongues. According to Magliocco (2010), there is a rather strong relationship between folklore teaching, language, culture, and identity. In his study, Mzimela (129) underlines the need of teaching folklore to young children as early as possible since it provides them with information that explains the past and provides insight into a people's current state through the language they best understand. Storytelling is an interactive activity in which both the narrator and the listener actively participate. Teaching using tales may also be participatory. Here the teacher and the learners interact freely. Interaction can also happen among the learners themselves (Mahanand 79). Moreover, the National Curriculum Framework (2005) recommends the use of students' local language, traditions, skills including tales and proverbs in the textbooks. Providing children with the home environment is definitely needed to stimulate an interest to learn. NEP 2020 also emphasis the traditional Indian knowledge including tribal and other local knowledge, across the humanities, sciences, arts, crafts and sports will be included in the curriculum. Stories are a potent medium to achieve this as they promote moral values for peaceful coexistence. By teaching learners through traditional stories we can enrich their experience in class with the precious wealth of knowledge related to Indian culture and heritage. Thus, folktales have a very important role to play in fostering children's socio-emotional and language development, as well as fostering cultural identity of individuals and growth of nation.

Discussion and Conclusion

Traditional tribal folktales hold significant educational value by offering unique insights and learning opportunities across various aspects of education. They serve as a means of cultural preservation, transmitting heritage and fostering a sense of identity while exposing students to diverse worldviews. Folktales provide moral and ethical lessons that help in character development, while their rich narratives encourage critical thinking, creativity, and imagination. They also contribute to language preservation, enhance literacy skills, and support social and emotional learning by fostering empathy and conflict resolution skills. Additionally, folktales promote environmental awareness and can be integrated across various subjects for a holistic, interdisciplinary approach to education, nurturing the intellectual, emotional, and social growth of students. At present century, the practice of storytelling and folktales is disappearing due to easier access for children to digital entertainment, less interest among children in regards to in traditional stories in general, less parent-child-family interaction in modern family households, and limited scope for folktales in the school curricula of different schools. To ensure that children are not deprived of the valuable lessons and morals that are found in many folktales, more concrete steps need to be taken to ensure that the practice of storytelling is protected, along with the archiving as well as continuation of narration of age-appropriate folktales and parents and teachers both have a very critical role to play in this regard (Sarwar). Folktales provide valuable insights into ethical practices, sustainability, and responsible consumption across various vocations. Through these stories, students can learn about the significance of environmental preservation, fair trade, and the value of all life forms (Cynthiya & Bhuvaneswari, 167). Folktales are not just meant to be heard and enjoyed; they carry strong messages. The characters often reflect human traits, and it is essential to discern the underlying moral lessons embedded within these stories. Early school education is the most important period of character formation as education and memories of this period is a gateway to the personality of an individual. Introduction of folktales in this stage can work as an excellent tool to teach cultural values, however, it cannot be denied that moral lessons and ethical values are needed to be learnt and practiced by people of all ages. Folktales, as a subject, might be an effective moral education at all levels of education instruction because they instill a strong sense of cultural and social belonging.

References

Abdalrahman, K.K., "Teaching and learning vocabulary through short stories", *Canadian Journal of Language and Literature Studies,* 2022, 2(2), 7-15.

Amali, H.I., "The function of folktales as a process of educating children in the 21st century: A case study of Idoma folktales", *21st Century Academic Forum Conference Proceedings IC21CE 2014 in Dubai,* 2014, Vol. 2, No. 1.

Chiparausha, Blessing, and Frederick Mavhunduse, "The role of folktales in the preservation of indigenous knowledge among the Shona: A review based on Aaron C. Hodza's Ngano Dzamatambidzanwa." *Southern African Journal for Folklore Studies* 24.2 (2014): 207-219.

Cynthiya, Rose J.S., and Bhuvaneswari, R. "Folktales from sir continents: Cultural influence and life skill development for children." Journal of Language and Literary Studies, 165-177.

Dahal, H. & Bhatta, B., "Folktales: A moral message from the past to the future generation", *Nepal Journal of Multidisciplinary Research (NJMR*), March 2021, Vol. 4, No. 1.

Dorji, T. C., "Preserving Our Folktales, Myths and Legends in the Digital Era." *Storytelling, Self, Society*, 2010, 6(1), 19–38. http://www.jstor.org/stable/41949038

Dung, N.T., "The world of Fantasy in Vietnamese folk Tales" (Survey, Research). *Writers' Association Publisher,* (2017).

Ihalagama, S., Culture Communication Through Folktale Practices Among School Children Toward Child Socialization, 2019.

Lall, Pragya, "Nurturing Skills through Narratives: Exploring anonymous folktales from India for Vocational and Skill Education." (2023).

Mahanand, Anand, "Role of traditional stories for English language education." Fortell, 42, 74-83.

Mishra, Krushna Chandra, "Folk-Songs of Arunachal Pradesh: The Thrust on Beauty and Love." *Lokaratna* 4 (2011).

Mzimela, J., "Exploring the role of teaching using folklore in developing grade R learners' Mother tongue", *Kamla-Raj,* 2016, Vol. 14, Issue 2.

Rajeshwari, R., "History preservation and folk literature – A study."

Saad, Sharina, "The Semai folktales cultural heritage in the 21st century: Preservation through innovation." *Journal of Educational Research and Indigeneous Studies* 2.1 (2019).

Sayeef, A., "Teaching English language using popular folktales in Bangladesh", *International Journal of Literature, Linguistics and Language Teaching,* January 2019, Vol. 1, Issue 1.

Samson- Akpan, E.S., "Ibibio Folktales in Education". *Nigeria Magazine*, 1986, Vol. 54, No. 4. Lagos. NCAC. 67-74.

Smith, A.B. & Johnson, L.M., "The impact of storytelling on cultural preservation", *Journal of Heritage Tourism*, 2019, 14(4), 356-369.

Suwanpratest, O., "An Analysis of the Prominent Cultural Values of Asian People through Similar Folktales." *International Journal of Social Science and Humanity*, Vol. 6, No. 11, 2016, pp. 836-839.

Quy, N.T.T., & Phuong, L.T., "The importance of fairy tales in communication, education, and cultural preservation", *International Journal of Social Science and Human Research*, October 2023, Vol. 06, Issue 10.

Chapter - 13

Status of Implementation of NEP 2020 in Arunachal Pradesh with Special Reference to School Education

– Mumni Tayeng & Dr. Sushant Kumar Nayak

Abstract

The National Education Policy, 2020 endeavours to articulate the nation's developmental requirements. In order to expand on India's ancient knowledge system and develop an educational system that is in line with 21st-century goals, particularly SDG4, the policy has proposed revisions and overhauls to every component of the educational framework. Arunachal Pradesh is one of the states that is working hard for proper implementation of the new vision of the policy. The paper is an attempt to explore the status of implementation of NEP, 2020 with special reference to school education. The policy put special emphasis on Early Childhood Care and Education, (ECCE) and Foundational Literacy and Numeracy (FLN) as strong bases for future schooling and lifelong learning. The upcoming times for ECCE seems positive as there has been establishment of 840 ECCE centres throughout the state. The NIPUN Bharat Mission was launched to attain FLN of children the Foundational Learning Study (FLS) conducted in Arunachal Pradesh allows to make provisions to improve the FLN. For Foundational Literacy, the result revealed 33% exceeds Global Minimum Proficiency, 29% partially meets Global Minimum Proficiency, 20% Meets Global Minimum Proficiency and 18% were Below partially meets Global minimum proficiency. The results for Foundational Numeracy exhibited 49% partially meets Global Minimum Proficiency, 37% Meets Global Minimum Proficiency, 8% were Below partially meets Global minimum proficiency, 6% exceeds Global Minimum Proficiency. These results can be interpreted that the children of Arunachal Pradesh studying in Grade III have better Foundational Literacy than Foundational Numeracy.

Key Words: NEP 2020, School Education, ECCE, FLN, Arunachal Pradesh.

Introduction

Education is the fundamental asset that helps in the achievement of harmonious and full development of a human being- physical, mental and spiritual. Education is a tool to create a more just and equal society, improve the quality of life, and advance national progress. From time immemorial, Education has proven to be a valuable asset in the life and culture of India. Ensuring that every person has access to high-quality education is essential to India's continuous rise to prominence in the world economy, social justice and equality, science, national integration, and cultural preservation. Education therefore, serves as a one of the major prospective of social change and national development. India is a treasure trove of exceptional and unique talent and high-quality universal education can elevate the talents and resources of the youth at maximum potential. A carefully thought-out and well implemented education system could enable the child to realise their greatest potential. The National Eduction Policy (NEP), 2020 aims to meet the nation's numerous and expanding developmental imperatives including the Sustainable Developmental Goals 4 (SDGs)- "Ensure inclusive and equitable quality education and promote lifelong learning opportunities for all" as well as focusing on enhancing the tradition custom and value system of India. The implementation of NEP, 2020 will bring a paradigm shift in the approach of educationist and all stakeholders.

Arunachal Pradesh had a late start in the sector of education. The tribal people of Arunachal Pradesh were left with "let alone" policy leading to huge lag and gap in comparison to other people of the nation. Only after gaining independence did the Government of India took significant action in the area of formal education. With a literacy rate of 66.95 % (census, 2011) Arunachal Pradesh is making rapid strides towards bridging the gap in education sector. The state today has over 4000 schools, compared to just 3 elementary schools at the time of independence. As Arunachal Pradesh is a state comprising a cumulation of different tribes, the scheduled tribe students may find the school education irrelevant to their culture. The tribal students often face disadvantages due to geographical or historical factors. The NEP, 2020 has put huge emphasis on "Learning for all" with equitable and Inclusive education. Promotion of Inclusive education can help in bridging the gap between the people of Arunachal Pradesh and mainstream education. The state government has pledged to phase-in the implementation of NEP, 2020 one of the greatest reforms in the educational sector—by 2030. Nonetheless, the state government acknowledged that putting a new policy into effect is difficult. Implementation of any policy can be successful when there will be full involvement of all stakeholders.

School Education

School Education in India followed a 10+2 structure. The NEP, 2020 replaced that system with a new 5+3+3+4 pedagogical and curricular structure. The details of the new structure are -

(A) **Foundational (5 years)**- it is further divided into 3 years of Anganwadi/pre-primary/Balvatika for children of age 3-6. From age 6 to 8, the children will attend classes 1&2.

(B) **Preparatory (3 years)**- for children aged 8-11 and they can unroll in classes 3 to 5.

(C) **Middle (3 years)**- It consist of classes 6 to 8 for children of the age group 11-14.

(D) **Secondary (4 years)**- the final stage of the ne education policy conceit of 4 years. It starts from class 9 upto 12. The children shall belong to 14-18 age group.

According to the NEP, 2020 School education should emphasis on development of various skills in the child-

1. **Cognitive Skills: -**

   (a) Foundational skill of Literacy and Numeracy.

(b) Higher order skill like critical thinking and problem solving.

2. **Soft Skills:-** Social and Emotional Skills which includes cultural awareness, empathy, teamwork, communication etc.

School Education should also focus its attention to the following points:-

1. Establishment of primary schools to help increase access to education.
2. Merging various small schools, where the enrolment of students is very low, to form a school network for efficient governance.
3. Emphasis of quality education that is mind crafting, character building as well as provide positive impact on citizenship.
4. Quality education can be ensured with the transformation of current education system, curriculum and pedagogy with 5+3+3+4 structure. The examination and assessment system should also be reformed while also focusing on strengthening the area of teacher education and training.

The NEP, 2020 aims and aspire to universalise the pre-primary education (Early Childhood Care and Education, ECCE) and provide special emphasis on attainment of Foundational Literacy and Numeracy (FLN). The current paper attempts to identify the status of implementing the above two aims in Arunachal Pradesh with regard to School education as envisioned in National Education Policy, 2020.

- **Early Childhood Care and Education, (ECCE)**

Early childhood is the period that starts from birth upto 8 years of age. It includes physical, socio-emotional, cognitive and motor development of the child. It had regarded as critical period of life and rapid brain development, foundational health and well being are laid. Many research have repeatedly shown that a child can improve subsequently with early childhood development programmes and opportunities for early learning. Early Childhood care and Education

(ECCE) aims to enable the child to build their skills, promotion of early learning that will support the children for lifetime. Arunachal Pradesh has launched the 'Mission Shiksha- Year of education, 2021' in order to improve and strengthen the education sector. Under it's flagship the state saw an increase in the number of schools (3,603) with 840 Early Childhood Care and Education centres established under Samara Shiksha. The establishment of the ECCEs helps in increasing the access to education in Arunachal Pradesh. There is also a significant increase in the pre-primary education classes from 3% in 2016 to 27% in 2022. The ECCE are delivered through Anganwadi centres. In Arunachal Pradesh, the functioning of Anganwadi centres and supervision of Anganwadi workers are under the Integrated Child Development Services Scheme (ICDS). The data from the Foundational Learning Study, 2022 shows that 83% students of class 3 have attended pre-primary school/Anganwadi centres. It also reported that 50% of the schools have pre-primary/ Anganwadi centre.

- **Foundational Literacy and Numeracy (FLN)**

Foundational Literacy and Numeracy (FLN) is the basic ability to read and write and perform basic operations with numbers. It is a significant and crucial foundation for the future schooling and lifelong learning. Hence, universal acquisition of FLN is one of the highest priorities aim of NEP, 2020. In order to assure that every child is able to attain FLN at the end of Grade III by 2026-27, the Government of India has launched a national mission under Samara Shiksha on 5th July, 2021. The mission is known as 'National Initiative for Proficiency in Reading with Understanding and Numeracy' (NIPUN Bharat). It is a 5-tier implementation mechanism that involves roles and responsibilities at 5 levels. They are-

1. National- Head: Secretary (DoSE&L)
2. State/UT - Head: Secretary Education
3. District- Head: DC/DM/CEO Zila Parishad
4. Block/Cluster
5. School and Community

The Foundational Learning Study is a report that provides insights into the learning level in FLN, interventions and follow ups for overall improvement in the system. The data derived from the study provided a baseline for NIPUN Bharat Mission. According to UDISE+ 2020-21, Arunachal Pradesh has a total of 3,483 schools with Grade III. For the FLN study, 107 schools, 193 teachers and a total of 1,237 students' participation was recorded. The components of the study are of two parts: -

1. Foundational Literacy

It is the ability to read, write and communicate in a particular language. The language used for the assessment in the state was English.

Table 1: Sub-Tasks of Foundational Literacy, FLS State Report, Arunachal Pradesh

Sub-Task	Meaning	Result
Oral Language Comprehension	The ability to understand the meaning of language (through spoken stories or pictures)	The Average performance was 85% which was similar to National average performance. On a scale of 0 to 5, Arunachal Pradesh recoded an aggregated performance of 4 similar to national aggregate.
Phonological awareness	The ability to identify sounds within a given word	On a scale of 0 to 12, the aggregated performance was 9 while the national aggregate was 10.
Decoding Letters	The ability to sound out the symbols (akshara or letters)	On a scale of 0 to 100, the aggregated performance was 95 while the national aggregate was 94.
Decoding Words	The ability to sound out grade-level real words	On a scale of 0 to 50, the aggregated performance was 38 while the national aggregate was 40.
Decoding Non-words	The ability to sound out non-words by identifying each symbol's (akshara or letter) sound	On a scale of 0 to 50, the aggregated performance was 33 while the national aggregate was 36.
Picture Matching	The ability to understand the meaning of written text	On a scale of 0 to 5, the aggregated performance was 5 while the national aggregate was 4.

Benchmark of Oral Reading Fluency (ORF) and comprehension	Reading aloud two grade appropriate short stories and answering questions related to retrieval and inferences.	• 18% were Below partially meets Global minimum proficiency while national average was 17%. • 29% partially meets Global Minimum Proficiency while national average was also 29%. • 20% Meets Global Minimum Proficiency while national average was 21%. • 33% exceeds Global Minimum Proficiency while national average was also 33%.

2. Foundational Numeracy

It comprises of the ability to understand numbers, perform basic operations with numbers and apply the understanding of patterns and numbers in real life situations.

Table 2: Sub-Tasks of Foundational Numeracy, FLS State Report, Arunachal Pradesh

Sub-Task	Meaning	Result
Number identification	The task was based on recognising and reading aloud numbers (up to 9999).	On a scale from 0 to 24, the aggregated performance was 20 while the national average was 19.
Number discrimination	The task comprised of comparing pairs of numbers to identify the bigger number.	On a scale from 0 to 14, the aggregated performance was 12 while the national average was also 12.
Number operation (addition and subtraction)	The task was based on completing addition and subtraction facts.	On a scale from 0 to 8, the aggregated performance was 6 while the national average was also 6.
Number operation (Word Problems)	The task was based on solving word problems based on the operation of addition and subtraction.	On a scale from 0 to 6, the aggregated performance was 4 while the national average was also 4.
Number operations (Multiplication)	The task was based on Constructing and using multiplication facts (tables) of numbers 2 to 10 and using division facts	On a scale from 0 to 4, the aggregated performance was 3 while the national average was also 3.
Number operations (Division)	The task was based on Constructing and using multiplication facts (tables) of numbers 2 to 10 and using division facts.	On a scale from 0 to 4, the aggregated performance was 2 while the national average was 3.

Measurement (Calendar Reading)	The task comprised of solving word problems based on measurement and estimation of volume, length and time using standard and non-standard units	On a scale from 0 to 3, the aggregated performance was 2 while the national average was also 2.
Measurement (Volume)	The task comprised of solving word problems based on measurement and estimation of volume, length and time using standard and non-standard units	On a scale from 0 to 3, the aggregated performance was 2 while the national average was also 2.
Measurement (Time on clock)	The task comprised of solving word problems based on measurement and estimation of volume, length and time using standard and non-standard units	On a scale from 0 to 3, the aggregated performance was 2 while the national average was also 2.
Measurement (Length)	The task comprised of solving word problems based on measurement and estimation of volume, length and time using standard and non-standard units	On a scale from 0 to 3, the aggregated performance was 2 while the national average was 3.
Fractions	The task was based on identifying and representing fraction values of half, one-fourth, three-fourth of a whole and in a collection of 12 objects.	On a scale from 0 to 6, the aggregated performance was 3 while the national average was also 3.
Patterns	The task comprised of identifying and extending patterns comprising of numbers and shapes	On a scale from 0 to 8, the aggregated performance was 6 while the national average was also 6.
Data Handling	The task was based on reading simple display of data and answering questions based on the data display.	On a scale from 0 to 6, the aggregated performance was 4 while the national average was 5.
Benchmark of Numeracy and Student Performance		• 8% were Below partially meets Global minimum proficiency while national average was 11%. • 49% partially meets Global Minimum Proficiency while national average was 37%.
		• 37% Meets Global Minimum Proficiency while national average was 42%. • 6% exceeds Global Minimum Proficiency while national average was 10%.

The Foundational Learning Study offers information on FLN's learning level as well as interventions and follow-ups for systemic enhancement. From the tables, an assumption can be made that the students of Arunachal Pradesh studying in Grade III have better Foundational Literacy in comparison to Foundational Numeracy.

Conclusion

NEP, 2020 is regarded as one of the greatest reforms in the system of education. It envisions to develop a good human being who is capable of rational thought and action, is compassionate, empathetic as well as courageous and resilient. It gave a new design of 5+3+3+4 to restructure the school curriculum and pedagogy. With a focus on school education and its first two aims, the paper concludes with the status of implementation of NEP, 2020 in Arunachal Pradesh. The ECCE is an integral part of NEP, 2020 that envisage the importance of Early childhood care as a foundation for the future. The FLN is a crucial precondition which will also serve as a foundation for the future schooling or life-long learning. The Government of India, State Government as well as all stakeholders are working jointly for proper implementation of the New Education Policy. The new design of 5+3+3+4 structure is yet to unfurl state wide but step by step implementation of NEP, 2020 is the pledge of the Government of Arunachal Pradesh.

References

"Arunachal to implement NEP by 2030, says CM." Arunachal Observer, 18 June. 2022. 19 February. 2024. Web. < https://arunachalobserver.org/2022/06/18/arunachal-to-implement-nep-by-2030-says-cm/>

Arunachal Pradesh, Lohit District, "District ICDS cell." February 2. 2024, https://lohit.nic.in/district-icds-cell/

India, Ministry of Human Resource Development, "New Education Policy, 2020." 2020,

https://www.education.gov.in/sites/upload_files/mhrd/files/NEP_Final_English_0.pdf ndia, Ministry of Education. "New Education Policy, 2020." September 1. 2023, https://www.education.gov.in/nep/aboutnep#:~:text=In%20school%20education%2C%20the%20National,solving%20%E2%80%93%20but%20also%2C%20social%20and India, My GOV.

"Arunachal Pradesh's Mission Youth – Bolstering Education with Mission Shiksha." November 22. 2023, https://blog.mygov.in/arunachal-pradeshs-mission-youth-bolstering-education-with-mission-shiksha/

India, Ministry of Education, National Council of Educational Research & Training, "FLS 2022 State Report: Arunachal Pradesh." NCERT, 2022. https://nipunbharat.education.gov.in/fls/file/state/arunachal_pradesh.pdf

India, Ministry of Education, Department of School Education & Literacy, "NIPUN Bharat Mission, Stakeholders: Roles and Responsibilities." 18 May. 2023, https://dsel.education.gov.in/sites/default/files/update/NIPUN_Bharat_stakeholders_roles_responsibilities.pdf

India, Ministry of Education, Department of School Education & Literacy, "NIPUN Bharat (FLN)." 18 May, 2023, https://dsel.education.gov.in/nipun-bharat

India, National Council of Educational Research & Training, "New Education Policy, 2020, Early Childhood Care and Education (ECCE): Foundations of Learning, https://www.education.gov.in/shikshakparv/docs/background_note_ECCE.pdf

Saroh, T., *Education in North-East India.* Kumud Publications. New Delhi (India), 2015. Print.

Sharma, V. and Parul., "Implementation Challenges of National Education Policy-2020 with reference to Higher Education: Some Suggestions". *University News*. 61 (2023): 30-34. Print.

Index

N